The G.L.A.D.S. Method

for

Cultivating Gratitude

A gratitude journal designed to take you from
feeling grateful to *being* grateful

Dr. Malorie Schneider

ISBN 979-8-218-33314-0 (HC)
ISBN 979-8-218-3604403 (eBook)

Disclaimer: The content provided is for educational, informational, and entertainment purposes only. Nothing found in this book is intended to be a substitute for professional therapeutic, psychological, or medical advice. If you are in need of mental health services, please contact a licensed professional in your area.

This Journal Belongs To:

_____

Year:_____

Contents

Welcome!

Welcome to The G.L.A.D.S. Method for Cultivating Gratitude.

I am so happy you are holding this journal, and I am excited about the journey on which you are about to embark. Whether you purchased this journal for yourself or it was given to you, this will surely be a gift in your life and the lives of those with whom you come in contact.

Before we get started, I would like to introduce myself. My name is Dr. Malorie Schneider. I am a licensed clinical psychologist residing in the beautiful state of Florida. I am incredibly blessed to have a career that is also my passion—helping others become who they were meant to be. I am married to my best friend, John, and we enjoy traveling, outdoor activities, and playing with our two spunky Hungarian Pulik—also known as the "dreadlock dog" breed. I have two wonderful adult children, Jeremy and Jacqueline, who taught me so much about unconditional love, playfulness, and joy.

I am abundantly grateful, but this has not always been the case. There was a period in my life when I felt empty, alone, unloved, and discouraged. I was succeeding in my academics and was very involved with raising my two young children, and from the outside, it looked like I was doing great; but I was struggling to *feel* okay. I was in graduate school at the time, and psychology researchers had just begun to study the role of spirituality, including gratitude, on psychological well-being. The research showed that individuals who kept a gratitude journal experienced improved mood. Being empirically driven, I decided to give it a try. I bought a cloth-covered journal and committed to writing down three things each evening for which I was grateful. This was not always easy. There were days I struggled to find three things to write down, but I kept to my commitment. Little by little, I began to notice a change in me, and the positive things started to stand out to me much more than the negative. I began to feel lighter, more hopeful, and at peace. It has been over 25 years since I started my first gratitude journal, and I continue to keep a daily gratitude journal because it works!

From my personal and professional experience, I know gratitude changes everything. For decades I have encouraged my patients to keep a gratitude journal as part of their wellness journey. After years of explaining to my patients the what, why, and how of a gratitude journal and hearing positive feedback on the impact of keeping a gratitude journal, I was inspired to take my concept of a gratitude journal to a broader audience so that others could experience the great change that gratitude has on one's life.

Why gratitude?

Certainly, you have had moments in which you felt warm and happy as you experienced gratitude for something or someone. We all know when we feel good, we feel good. But did you know that you are changing your brain each time you feel and express gratitude? Writing down gratitudes increases activation in the medial prefrontal cortex of your brain—the part involved in learning and decision-making. What's more is that this sensitivity continues, meaning that practicing gratitude trains your brain to be more sensitive to the experience of gratitude, which in turn can contribute to improved mental health over time. Pretty neat stuff, right? But wait, there's more. Gratitude has been shown to increase the number of relationships, improve physical health, enhance empathy, reduce aggression, improve sleep, increase self-esteem, reduce stress, and even help overcome trauma. Need I say more about why the practice of gratitude is so life-changing?

What is a GLADS journal?

My first method for keeping a gratitude journal was to write down three specific things I was grateful for each day and why. Sometimes writing the gratitude entries was a simple act, and other times I really struggled to find anything to write down in my journal for that day. I found that when I struggled at the end of the day to identify three gratitudes, I was "more on the lookout" for gratitudes the next day so my journaling would be easier. This "being on the lookout" translated into getting a double benefit because not only was I acknowledging the gratitudes at the end of the day, I was actively seeking them out throughout the day. I started to approach each day expecting to find things for which to be grateful. And, to be honest with you, this is what got me through a difficult period of my life. I found that even on the most dreary, challenging days, I could still find some positive things...even if one of those things was as small as being grateful that all of the traffic lights stayed green on my way to school that day!

As wonderful as it was to keep a gratitude journal, eventually, I felt I needed something more, something different. So over the years, I expanded and revised my approach to a gratitude journal from writing down three gratitudes each day to what you are now holding, the GLADS Method. What is in the world is the GLADS method? **GLADS** is an acronym that expands and focuses your gratitude by helping you identify gratitudes, learnings, accomplishments, delights, and self-care (see below). The most significant benefits of keeping a gratitude journal are a result of daily journaling, and I want you to get as much benefit out of this practice as possible. Therefore, this book is designed as a daily gratitude journal. If you are starting this journal the last wekk of December, begin with week 52; start with whatever week of the year you are in. Each week there is a quote accompanied by a story of encouragement and inspiration intended to provoke self-examination and self-discovery and open your eyes to areas of gratitude you may not have yet found. You will then have space to complete your daily GLADS. Additionally, you will review your daily GLADS entries at the end of each week and create your weekly "Top GLADS" entry. You will also find spaces in this journal to engage in mindfulness coloring--have fun!

The GLADS Method

GLADS is an acronym for Grateful, Learned, Accomplished, Delighted, Self-Care. In this journal you will find the **GLADS** acronym. After each letter of the acronym, write down one specific thing for which you were Grateful, something you Learned, something you Accomplished, something that Delighted you, and what you did for Self-care.

Grateful: Identify one thing you were grateful for and why.

Learned: Something you learned—a new skill, a personal insight, relationship insight, etc.

Accomplished: What did you accomplish? Some days this might be a milestone, while other days, this may be "I got showered and dressed." No judgment. If you had to push to do something—it is an accomplishment!

Delighted: What "tickled" you? What brought you joy? This is anything—hot cocoa, a funny joke, sunshine, blowing bubbles, a compliment you gave or received, etc.

Self-care: How did you take care of yourself? You are important and worthy of love and caring. If you did not do self-care, write down what you will do and then do it!

Example:

G: Today I am grateful for the beautiful sunrise I saw on my run. It reminded me of how blessed I am to live near the ocean.

L: I learned that taking a short walk mid-day rejuvenates my mind and spirit.

A: I accomplished going to bed when my body felt tired instead of staying up and watching t.v.

D: I was delighted to catch up with a dear friend.

S: I engaged in box breathing during my daytime walk

How will you know this is working for you?

I have created the 3A's for tracking your personal progress: Aware, Assess, Affirm. You will have space to track your progress at the end of each week and then at the end of each month.

1. **A**ware is designed for you to non-judgmentally review your week/month and simply note what stands out to you about the week—Did you miss the mark for engaging in self-care as often as you hoped? Were you inconsistent in your GLADS daily entries? Were gratitudes over-flowing? Whatever you notice, jot it down, and anything that may have positively or negatively influenced what you noticed.

2. **A**ssess is designed for you to assign a measurable value to how you felt over the past week/month. You will use a 1-10 scale, with ten being the most positive, to rate how you felt physically, emotionally, relationally, and overall. Finally, you will assess your overall level of gratitude for the past week. These scores will provide you with feedback on where you are doing great and on where you can focus for improvement. We can't change what we don't know!

3. **A**ffirm is designed for you to positively acknowledge anything about yourself for the past week/month. This affirmation can be as simple as, "Great job! I completed all of my daily GLADS this week...even when I was tired," or, "It was a week full of challenges, and I took the time to assess where I currently am. Good job!" or, "Wow! My level of gratitude has gone up from last month."

There is no right or wrong way to use this journal. Consistency, though, is key. You will find that in the brightest of times and in the darkest of times, there is always something to be grateful for, something to be learned, something you accomplish (even if it is just getting through), something delightful, and always a reason to take good care of you.

Welcome to your gratitude journey!

Week One
The Gift of Gratitude

Feeling gratitude and not expressing it is like wrapping a present and not giving it.

William Arthur Ward

The gift-giving holidays are now over, and we are embarking upon a new year with new hopes, goals, and a sense of excitement at beginning anew. While gift-giving is still fresh in your mind, take a moment to reflect on the gift-giving process. You carefully selected a gift, knowing how much the receiver would love and appreciate it. Then it was beautifully wrapped and given to your loved one. You waited anxiously to witness the joy your gift would bring that special person. As you watched them open the present, you remarkably experienced joy at their joy. Would you or that special person have felt joy if you had purchased the gift but failed to give it to them? Of course not! Gifts allow us to feel connected with someone we care about, and gratitude is among the greatest gifts we can give. Today, identify someone you are grateful for and then tell that person why you are grateful to have him/her in your life.

Week One
GLADS

Monday

G _____

L _____

A _____

D _____

S _____

Tuesday

G _____

L _____

A _____

D _____

S _____

Week One
GLADS

Wednesday

G _____

L _____

A _____

D _____

S _____

Thursday

G _____

L _____

A _____

D _____

S _____

GLADS

Friday

G _____

L _____

A _____

D _____

S _____

Saturday

G _____

L _____

A _____

D _____

S _____

Sunday

G _____

L _____

A _____

D _____

S _____

"Top GLADS" for this week:

G _____

L _____

A _____

D _____

S _____

Aware:

Use the space below to review your week nonjudgmentally. What did you notice in your gratitude practice? Where did you do great? Where can you improve? What were the obstacles? What were the "wins"?

Assess:

Score yourself in each area below on a 1-10 scale, with 10 being "top notch!"

Physical	Emotional	Relational	Overall
_____	_____	_____	_____

Goals or ideas for improving in any of these areas:

Affirm:

Use the space below to positively acknowledge and affirm anything about yourself or your efforts from this past week:

Week Two

Compassion

If you want others to be happy, practice compassion. If you want to be happy, practice compassion.

--Dalai Lama

How does one practice compassion? First, let's look at what compassion is. At its core, compassion means "to suffer along with." Compassion is different from having pity or sympathy for someone. Merriam-Webster defines compassion as "a sympathetic consciousness of others' distress together with a desire to alleviate it." The research literature on compassion takes this definition one step further to include not just having a desire to alleviate others' distress but also taking some kind of movement toward easing that pain. This action step does not mean we move right in and "fix" whatever is "wrong." This type of response comes from a place of our own discomfort with pain and a faulty belief that we are somehow "better than" and we can "fix" what is "wrong." Trying to "fix" what is "wrong" leads to a greater sense of separation and disconnection that can add to the person's distress. Instead, compassion is recognizing that we are all equals in that we all experience pain and what action we most need is the act of someone just being with us. I believe there is no greater suffering than feeling alone in our pain. American author Fredrick Buechner put it this way:

"Compassion is sometimes the fatal capacity for feeling what it is like to live inside somebody else's skin. It is the knowledge that there can never really be any peace and joy for me until there is peace and joy finally for you too."

This week, be mindful of how compassion shows up. Are you compassionate towards yourself? Towards others? Did you have the opportunity to observe compassion? How did this feel?

GLADS

Monday

G _____

L _____

A _____

D _____

S _____

Tuesday

G _____

L _____

A _____

D _____

S _____

GLADS

Wednesday

G _____

L _____

A _____

D _____

S _____

Thursday

G _____

L _____

A _____

D _____

S _____

Week Two

GLADS

Friday

G _____

L _____

A _____

D _____

S _____

Saturday

G _____

L _____

A _____

D _____

S _____

GLADS

Sunday

G _____

L _____

A _____

D _____

S _____

"Top GLADS" for this week:

G _____

L _____

A _____

D _____

S _____

Aware:

Use the space below to review your week nonjudgmentally. What did you notice in your gratitude practice? Where did you do great? Where can you improve? What were the obstacles? What were the "wins"?

Assess:

Score yourself in each area below on a 1-10 scale, with 10 being "top notch!"

Physical	Emotional	Relational	Overall
_____	_____	_____	_____

Goals or ideas for improving in any of these areas:

Affirm:

Use the space below to positively acknowledge and affirm anything about yourself or your efforts from this past week:

Week Three

Faith

Faith is taking the first step, even when you don't see the whole staircase.

-Martin Luther King, Jr

On January 15, 1929, Martin Luther King Jr was born the son of a Baptist minister in Atlanta, Georgia. No one knew who this baby would grow up to be, and I would guess that as a young teenager and even into adulthood, Martin Luther King Jr could not have fully anticipated the impact his life would have on an entire country. In 1955 he organized the first major protests of the African-American civil rights movement. He had faith in the belief that all were created equal. He may not have seen where this first step would lead, but he had faith and took that first step and then the next step and the next step until, in his final speech before his assassination, he declares, "Only when it is dark enough can we see the stars... And he's allowed me to go to the mountain. And I've looked over, and I've seen the Promised Land! I may not get there with you. But I want you to know tonight, that we, as a people, will get to the promised land!

Taking that first step when the journey is unclear can be so difficult, but if we don't take that first step, we will never see whatever that "Promised Land" is for us. Be brave. Have faith. Feel the fear and take that first step just the same!

GLADS

Monday

G _____

L _____

A _____

D _____

S _____

Tuesday

G _____

L _____

A _____

D _____

S _____

GLADS

Wednesday

G _____

L _____

A _____

D _____

S _____

Thursday

G _____

L _____

A _____

D _____

S _____

GLADS

Friday

G _____

L _____

A _____

D _____

S _____

Saturday

G _____

L _____

A _____

D _____

S _____

Sunday

G _____

L _____

A _____

D _____

S _____

"Top GLADS" for this week:

G _____

L _____

A _____

D _____

S _____

Aware:

Use the space below to review your week nonjudgmentally. What did you notice in your gratitude practice? Where did you do great? Where can you improve? What were the obstacles? What were the "wins"?

Assess:

Score yourself in each area below on a 1-10 scale, with 10 being "top notch!"

Physical	Emotional	Relational	Overall
_____	_____	_____	_____

Goals or ideas for improving in any of these areas:

Affirm:

Use the space below to positively acknowledge and affirm anything about yourself or your efforts from this past week:

Week Four

Reset

Believe and act as if it were impossible to fail.

-Charles Kettering

We are approaching the end of the first month of the New Year; how are those New Year's resolutions? Statistics indicate that 90% of New Year's resolutions will have been broken by month's end. If you are falling into that statistic, why is that? Could it be that stinking thinking has kicked in, and you have begun to believe that you just can't do it? Maybe you have had a setback and see that as evidence that you can't do what you set out to do. Let's do a reset. How will it be different when you approach your resolutions with the fervent belief that you cannot fail? How would this belief affect your actions? When I hear the word "fail," I hear "First Attempt In Learning." What have you learned? Now apply that learning to your resolution and keep moving forward!

GLADS

Monday

G _____

L _____

A _____

D _____

S _____

Tuesday

G _____

L _____

A _____

D _____

S _____

Wednesday

G _____

L _____

A _____

D _____

S _____

Thursday

G _____

L _____

A _____

D _____

S _____

GLADS

Friday

G _____

L _____

A _____

D _____

S _____

Saturday

G _____

L _____

A _____

D _____

S _____

GLADS

Sunday

G _____

L _____

A _____

D _____

S _____

"Top GLADS" for this week:

G _____

L _____

A _____

D _____

S _____

Aware:

Use the space below to review your week nonjudgmentally. What did you notice in your gratitude practice? Where did you do great? Where can you improve? What were the obstacles? What were the "wins"?

Assess:

Score yourself in each area below on a 1-10 scale, with 10 being "top notch!"

Physical	Emotional	Relational	Overall
_____	_____	_____	_____

Goals or ideas for improving in any of these areas:

Affirm:

Use the space below to positively acknowledge and affirm anything about yourself or your efforts from this past week:

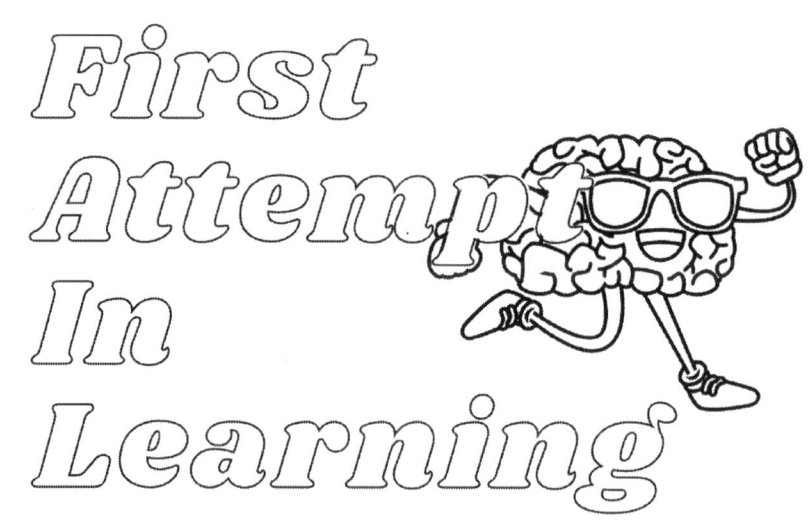

Week Five
Identity

When I let go of what I am, I become what I might be.

-Lao Tzu

Developmental psychologists stated that as early as four years of age, we have a sense of our identity. Who we believe ourselves to be is shaped by our social environment and continues to be shaped throughout our lifetime. Unfortunately, some of us hold on to "old identities" that no longer fit or that hold us back from discovering who we might be. If you have siblings, you are likely familiar with, "He's the athletic one, She's the pretty one, He's the funny one," etc. My role in the family was "the dependable one." I was the second oldest and the oldest female in a family of eight children. In many large families, the older children become second caregivers to the younger siblings. Since my older brother was "the forgetful one," and my sister, three and a half years younger than I, was "the pretty one," I was "the dependable one. " I had adult responsibilities, which I took very seriously and did an excellent job. I still maintain this identity as "the dependable one," and it has served me well throughout my life. However, it was not until my early thirties that I realized I am more than just "the dependable one." I am also intelligent, athletic, witty, attractive, competitive, and kind. I did not have to let go of being "the dependable one completely," but I did need to loosen my hold on that identity to make room for other aspects of me to emerge. The key to letting go of what you are so that you can become what you might be is opening yourself up to new experiences and different ways of thinking. I began running, even though my brother was "the runner," and I discovered that running is definitely me. I started noticing the uniqueness of my body shape and facial features and found that I am also pretty, just different from my sister, "the petite, pretty one." I could let go of my childhood identity of "the heavy one." I started going to theme parks and discovered I love thrills and adventures. Each year, I find other parts of me emerging while other aspects move more to the background, and still others I simply let go.

What old identities are you holding on to? Are you ready to let go so you can see what you can be?

Week Five
GLADS

Monday

G _____

L _____

A _____

D _____

S _____

Tuesday

G _____

L _____

A _____

D _____

S _____

GLADS

Wednesday

G _____

L _____

A _____

D _____

S _____

Thursday

G _____

L _____

A _____

D _____

S _____

Week Five
GLADS

Friday

G _____

L _____

A _____

D _____

S _____

Saturday

G _____

L _____

A _____

D _____

S _____

Sunday

G _____

L _____

A _____

D _____

S _____

"Top GLADS" for this week:

G _____

L _____

A _____

D _____

S _____

Aware:

Use the space below to review your week nonjudgmentally. What did you notice in your gratitude practice? Where did you do great? Where can you improve? What were the obstacles? What were the "wins"?

Assess:

Score yourself in each area below on a 1-10 scale, with 10 being "top notch!"

Physical	Emotional	Relational	Overall
_____	_____	_____	_____

Goals or ideas for improving in any of these areas:

Affirm:

Use the space below to positively acknowledge and affirm anything about yourself or your efforts from this past week:

FREE
YOURSELF
AND BE YOU!

Week Six

Gratitude for Challenges

We ought to give thanks for all fortune: if it is 'good,' because it is good, if 'bad' because it works in us patience, humility, and the contempt of this world and the hope of our eternal country.

-C.S. Lewis

Take a moment to review your past entries for what you were grateful for each day. Seriously. Stop reading and take a look and then come back.

If you are like almost every other person on this planet, I would guess that each thing you were grateful for would fall under the category of "good". That is our human nature—to be grateful for the positive in our lives. What is more difficult is to be grateful for the challenges in our lives. Now, take a moment to reflect on some of your challenges in life. I am willing to bet that at the time you wished things were different, that you did not have to be going through whatever it was. I am also willing to bet that when you look back at it now, you see how you grew in some positive way from that challenge.

Perhaps right now you are in the midst of one of those life challenges. If so, see if you can use your past experiences to find positive meaning in what you are going through. Today, be grateful for the opportunities life is handing you to grow. Be thankful for the person who speaks rudely to you for offering you the opportunity to learn patience, be grateful for the person who does something hurtful to you for the opportunity to practice forgiveness, and so on. While this is more difficult, especially in the moment, it also yields the highest reward in that we can have a grateful heart regardless of our circumstances.

Week Six
GLADS

Monday

G _____

L _____

A _____

D _____

S _____

Tuesday

G _____

L _____

A _____

D _____

S _____

Wednesday

G _____

L _____

A _____

D _____

S _____

Thursday

G _____

L _____

A _____

D _____

S _____

Friday

G _____

L _____

A _____

D _____

S _____

Saturday

G _____

L _____

A _____

D _____

S _____

Sunday

G _____

L _____

A _____

D _____

S _____

 "Top GLADS" for this week:

G _____

L _____

A _____

D _____

S _____

Aware:

Use the space below to review your week nonjudgmentally. What did you notice in your gratitude practice? Where did you do great? Where can you improve? What were the obstacles? What were the "wins"?

Assess:

Score yourself in each area below on a 1-10 scale, with 10 being "top notch!"

Physical	Emotional	Relational	Overall
_____	_____	_____	_____

Goals or ideas for improving in any of these areas:

Affirm:

Use the space below to positively acknowledge and affirm anything about yourself or your efforts from this past week:

Week Seven
Self-Love

To fall in love with yourself is the first secret to happiness.

-Robert Morley

When we think about Valentine's Day, we likely conjure up images of chocolates, roses, and romantic dinners. Perhaps you are a bit more cynical and think of Valentine's Day as nothing more than a day designed to make profits for card companies and florists. Valentine's Day, more formally referred to as Saint Valentine's Day, originated as a religious feast to honor two holy martyrs, both with the surname of Valentinus. One was a Roman priest and the other a bishop of Terni. Both were persecuted for their Christian beliefs and for performing wedding ceremonies for Roman soldiers, who were forbidden to marry. They both obtained the designation of a saint, and the Church designated Saint Valentine's Day as an official feast day in their honor. It was not until the 14th century that Valentine's Day became connected with romantic love as it is today. It is asserted that Chaucer, best known for his Canterbury Tales, wrote the poem The Parliament of Fowls. This poem is a debate between a parliament of birds regarding the nature and purpose of love. In the end, Nature encourages all of her birds to choose their appropriate mates and provides a promise that "even in the depths of winter, spring is not all that far off."

Today, you might be in the depths of your relationship winter, whether because you are alone or because your relationship is struggling, or you might be in the spring of your relationship.

Regardless of the season you are in relationally, make today your spring with yourself. Do something extraordinary for yourself today because your relationship with yourself is the most important human relationship in your life. If that relationship is healthy, then other relationships will follow.

GLADS

Monday

G _____

L _____

A _____

D _____

S _____

Tuesday

G _____

L _____

A _____

D _____

S _____

GLADS

Wednesday

G _____

L _____

A _____

D _____

S _____

Thursday

G _____

L _____

A _____

D _____

S _____

GLADS

Friday

G _____

L _____

A _____

D _____

S _____

Saturday

G _____

L _____

A _____

D _____

S _____

Sunday

G _____

L _____

A _____

D _____

S _____

"Top GLADS" for this week:

G _____

L _____

A _____

D _____

S _____

Aware:

Use the space below to review your week nonjudgmentally. What did you notice in your gratitude practice? Where did you do great? Where can you improve? What were the obstacles? What were the "wins"?

Assess:

Score yourself in each area below on a 1-10 scale, with 10 being "top notch!"

Physical	Emotional	Relational	Overall
_____	_____	_____	_____

Goals or ideas for improving in any of these areas:

Affirm:

Use the space below to positively acknowledge and affirm anything about yourself or your efforts from this past week:

Week Eight

Appreciation

The deepest craving of human nature is the need to be appreciated.-

-William James

William James is known as the Father of American Psychology and is rated as one of the top intellectual influencers of the twentieth century. He wrote and lectured on many topics, including radical empiricism, functionalism, religion, and free will. With those credentials, it is with seriousness that we consider what he saw as the "deepest craving of human nature": the need to be appreciated. Do you feel appreciated? How has keeping a GLADS journal helped you appreciate your wonderfulness? Whom do you appreciate? Just like feeling gratitude and not expressing it is like buying a gift and not giving it, so is feeling appreciation for someone or someone's kindness and not telling them.

Tune in to others today. Notice what they do for you and your life or how their existence makes this world a better place, and then express that appreciation. If possible, send a thank you note. How good does it feel to know you helped to satisfy someone's deepest craving?

Monday

G _____

L _____

A _____

D _____

S _____

Tuesday

G _____

L _____

A _____

D _____

S _____

Wednesday

G _____

L _____

A _____

D _____

S _____

Thursday

G _____

L _____

A _____

D _____

S _____

Friday

G _____

L _____

A _____

D _____

S _____

Saturday

G _____

L _____

A _____

D _____

S _____

Sunday

G _____

L _____

A _____

D _____

S _____

"Top GLADS" for this week:

G _____

L _____

A _____

D _____

S _____

Aware:

Use the space below to review your week nonjudgmentally. What did you notice in your gratitude practice? Where did you do great? Where can you improve? What were the obstacles? What were the "wins"?

Assess:

Score yourself in each area below on a 1-10 scale, with 10 being "top notch!"

Physical	Emotional	Relational	Overall
_____	_____	_____	_____

Goals or ideas for improving in any of these areas:

Affirm:

Use the space below to positively acknowledge and affirm anything about yourself or your efforts from this past week:

Week Nine

Perception

Change the way you look at things and the things you look at change.

-Wayne W. Dyer

In the early 1990s, Magic Eye ignited a worldwide 3D craze with posters called "jobbers." These 3D posters were created using a single-image stereogram designed to make the visual illusion of a three-dimensional scene from a two-dimensional image. These posters would line the kiosks in shopping malls, street fairs, and other places. People would stand staring at the posters and hear someone say, "I see it!" The person next to them would say, "Where? I don't see it. What is it?" And then, you would hear someone describe how to see the image by changing one's focus. Sometimes the other person would see it, and other times, they would finally give up. The key to "seeing" the 3D image in these posters is to overcome the normally automatic coordination between accommodation (focus) and horizontal vergence (angle of one's eyes). In regular sight, we see things through aligned vergence and accommodation, but for the image to "pop out," we must view it through parallel convergence, a different and "unnatural" way to view objects.

How have you been looking at things? Perhaps if you change how you look at things, something new and fascinating will pop up.

GLADS

Monday

G _____

L _____

A _____

D _____

S _____

Tuesday

G _____

L _____

A _____

D _____

S _____

GLADS

Wednesday

G _____

L _____

A _____

D _____

S _____

Thursday

G _____

L _____

A _____

D _____

S _____

Week Nine

GLADS

Friday

G _____

L _____

A _____

D _____

S _____

Saturday

G _____

L _____

A _____

D _____

S _____

Sunday

G _____

L _____

A _____

D _____

S _____

"Top GLADS" for this week:

G _____

L _____

A _____

D _____

S _____

Aware:

Use the space below to review your week nonjudgmentally. What did you notice in your gratitude practice? Where did you do great? Where can you improve? What were the obstacles? What were the "wins"?

Assess:

Score yourself in each area below on a 1-10 scale, with 10 being "top notch!"

Physical	Emotional	Relational	Overall

Goals or ideas for improving in any of these areas:

Affirm:

Use the space below to positively acknowledge and affirm anything about yourself or your efforts from this past week:

Week Ten
Spring Promises

In March, winter is holding back and spring is pulling forward. Something holds, and something pulls inside of us too.

-Jean Hersey

In some ways, March is the tug-of-war of nature. On one hand, it still possesses bitter winds and snow, and on the other hand, it delivers the first warm days of the new year with the promise of spring. It is the month when we need to have shorts and a sweatshirt in our closet as well as jeans and a coat. It can play with our hopes as we take joy in the warm weather, and just as quickly, the weather resumes the coldness to which we have become accustomed. Jean Hersey, a well-known gardener and author from Connecticut, highlights this same pull inside of us, wherein we are pulled towards something new and different, and yet we find ourselves holding to what we are used to.

I am presently experiencing this tug-of-war in my own life. The past year has been a bit of a personal winter. It has been filled with storms of all kinds, some beautiful even as they were occurring, and some only becoming beautiful once they quieted, and I could see what came with the storm and how things settled in a new and beautiful way after the storm. I can feel something holding me back, and yet there is a very strong pull to go forward. I can feel the excitement as I imagine the warmth that going forward will bring, and yet I have become accustomed to where I am. My familiarity with my current circumstances makes me want to stay in my "winter." Even as I have that thought, I feel a pull toward my "spring."

Every February 2, thousands of people and the news media gather at Gobbler's Knob in Punxsutawney, Pennsylvania, to see whether or not Punxsutawney Phil will see his shadow. According to legend, if Phil sees his shadow, we have six more weeks of winter. If he does not see his shadow, spring is just around the corner. While this has been a tradition for over 130 years, his predictive ability is less than perfect. A recent review found in the past decade, poor Phil only rates 40% accurately.

Regardless of what Phil predicted last month,perhaps this month, you can have your own type of"Groundhog Day," and rather than relying on a groundhog todetermine if you stay in winter or move on to spring, youtrust your inner wisdom, take the leap of faith and embracewhat "springs" forth.

Monday

G _____

L _____

A _____

D _____

S _____

Tuesday

G _____

L _____

A _____

D _____

S _____

Wednesday

G _____

L _____

A _____

D _____

S _____

Thursday

G _____

L _____

A _____

D _____

S _____

Friday

G _____

L _____

A _____

D _____

S _____

Saturday

G _____

L _____

A _____

D _____

S _____

Week Ten
GLADS

Sunday

G _____

L _____

A _____

D _____

S _____

"Top GLADS" for this week:

G _____

L _____

A _____

D _____

S _____

Aware:

Use the space below to review your week nonjudgmentally. What did you notice in your gratitude practice? Where did you do great? Where can you improve? What were the obstacles? What were the "wins"?

Assess:

Score yourself in each area below on a 1-10 scale, with 10 being "top notch!"

Physical	Emotional	Relational	Overall
_____	_____	_____	_____

Goals or ideas for improving in any of these areas:

Affirm:

Use the space below to positively acknowledge and affirm anything about yourself or your efforts from this past week:

Week Eleven
Future Past

Gratitude makes sense of our past, brings peace for today, and creates a vision for tomorrow

-Melody Beattie

One thing I know for sure is that our past is present in the present, and the present will be present in our future. For many, the past is unpleasantly impacting the here and now. This may be because of what others have done to us or because of the choices we made. Either way, we cannot change what happened in the past, but with a bit of work (or a lot of work), we can make peace with the past and maybe even find something positive to pull from the past.

We cannot time travel, at least not yet. But what if there were something you could do every day going forward that could help you create a better "future past"? Since our present will very soon become our past, living each moment of every day with gratitude will do exactly that! It is relatively simple to be grateful when things are going how we want, but being grateful for our challenges is, well, challenging. Today, identify something that has been challenging or unpleasant and then find a way to be grateful for it. Learning to be grateful in our toughest moments will surely make each moment a "good" moment that will then become a "good" past in the future.

GLADS

Monday

G _____

L _____

A _____

D _____

S _____

Tuesday

G _____

L _____

A _____

D _____

S _____

Wednesday

G _____

L _____

A _____

D _____

S _____

Thursday

G _____

L _____

A _____

D _____

S _____

GLADS

Friday

G _____

L _____

A _____

D _____

S _____

Saturday

G _____

L _____

A _____

D _____

S _____

Sunday

G _____

L _____

A _____

D _____

S _____

"Top GLADS" for this week:

G _____

L _____

A _____

D _____

S _____

Aware:

Use the space below to review your week nonjudgmentally. What did you notice in your gratitude practice? Where did you do great? Where can you improve? What were the obstacles? What were the "wins"?

Assess:

Score yourself in each area below on a 1-10 scale, with 10 being "top notch!"

Physical	Emotional	Relational	Overall
_____	_____	_____	_____

Goals or ideas for improving in any of these areas:

Affirm:

Use the space below to positively acknowledge and affirm anything about yourself or your efforts from this past week:

Week Twelve

Clutter

The objective of cleaning is not just to clean, but to feel happiness living in that environment.

-Marie Kondo

The vernal equinox, which typically falls on the 19th, 20th, or 21st day of March, is the instant of time when the plane of Earth's equator passes through the center of the sun. At this time, daytime and nighttime are of approximately equal duration all over the planet. For those of us in the northern hemisphere, this marks the first day of spring. It is a season marked by new beginnings as buds begin to push their way out of the winter-bare tree branches, tulip and daffodil sprouts shoot up from their buried bulbs, and the grass comes out of hibernation to reveal its green color once again. New energy and new life are all around us, and for many, we replicate nature's "out with the old, in with new" by starting our spring cleaning. I wonder what comes to mind when you think about spring cleaning. What is your reaction? Do you dread the process? Do you do it begrudgingly because you like the end result? Marie Kondo has recently become a media sensation with her hit show, Tidying Up. Her approach to cleaning and organization is Zen-like, and once you tune in to her, I would venture to say you will never think about cleaning in quite the same way. She brings joy and gratitude into the process of cleaning and organizing, and the end result is feeling happy in one's environment.

Marie Kondo is right. Research shows that a cluttered home is correlated with feelings of depression and fatigue and higher levels of the stress hormone cortisol. Clutter can also overwhelm the visual cortex making it more difficult to focus and concentrate.

I am a firm believer that one's environment reflects one's inner world and vice versa. Sometimes, it is easier to tidy up our bedroom than it is to sort through and tidy up our inner clutter, so start that spring cleaning and see how having a tidy home can bring you closer to inner peace.

Monday

G _____

L _____

A _____

D _____

S _____

Tuesday

G _____

L _____

A _____

D _____

S _____

Wednesday

G _____

L _____

A _____

D _____

S _____

Thursday

G _____

L _____

A _____

D _____

S _____

Friday

G _____

L _____

A _____

D _____

S _____

Saturday

G _____

L _____

A _____

D _____

S _____

Sunday

G _____

L _____

A _____

D _____

S _____

"Top GLADS" for this week:

G _____

L _____

A _____

D _____

S _____

Aware:

Use the space below to review your week nonjudgmentally. What did you notice in your gratitude practice? Where did you do great? Where can you improve? What were the obstacles? What were the "wins"?

Assess:

Score yourself in each area below on a 1-10 scale, with 10 being "top notch!"

Physical	Emotional	Relational	Overall
_____	_____	_____	_____

Goals or ideas for improving in any of these areas:

Affirm:

Use the space below to positively acknowledge and affirm anything about yourself or your efforts from this past week:

Week Thirteen

Kindness

Kindness in words creates confidence. Kindness in thinking creates profoundness. Kindness in giving creates love.

-Lao Tzu

Turn on the news, and within mere seconds you will hear harsh words being exchanged, close-minded opinions being touted, and cruel actions being taken. It can feel sad and hopeless. Yet, every once in a while, a news program will share a story of kindness that gives us joy and hope. I recently heard of a man finding a lost dog and driving across the country to return the dog to a young boy. I also heard of a fast food worker whose car finally broke down, and one of the regular customers had a son who had just purchased a new car and gave the worker his other car. These stories not only warm our hearts, but hopefully, they inspire us to be "that kind of a person."

The stories of kindness that make the news are big stories, but the smallest act of kindness can have as big of an impact as the largest act of kindness. How would you be different if you chose to view each situation with kindness? How would this change how you think and how you respond? How could a simple act of kindness impact someone else? Could you create a ripple effect of kindness?

Week Thirteen

GLADS

Monday

G _____

L _____

A _____

D _____

S _____

Tuesday

G _____

L _____

A _____

D _____

S _____

Wednesday

G _____

L _____

A _____

D _____

S _____

Thursday

G _____

L _____

A _____

D _____

S _____

Friday

G _____

L _____

A _____

D _____

S _____

Saturday

G _____

L _____

A _____

D _____

S _____

Sunday

G _____

L _____

A _____

D _____

S _____

"Top GLADS" for this week:

G _____

L _____

A _____

D _____

S _____

Aware:

Use the space below to review your week nonjudgmentally. What did you notice in your gratitude practice? Where did you do great? Where can you improve? What were the obstacles? What were the "wins"?

Assess:

Score yourself in each area below on a 1-10 scale, with 10 being "top notch!"

Physical	Emotional	Relational	Overall
_____	_____	_____	_____

Goals or ideas for improving in any of these areas:

Affirm:

Use the space below to positively acknowledge and affirm anything about yourself or your efforts from this past week:

Week Fourteen

Comparisons

Don't compare your situation to somebody else's. You're not running their race. You're running your own race.

-Joel Olsteen

I am competitive; I like to push myself to my very best and I like to win. For years I was a long distance runner. When training for a race, I would create a spreadsheet that showed the miles to run each day leading up to the race and then a place where I could enter my actual miles. As race day approached, the number of miles would increase and as number of miles increased, my average mile pace would decrease so that I would have the energy to sustain the longer distances. One day I was out for my prescribed 18 mile run. I had my course mapped out and I knew the pace I needed to run. At approximately the 3 mile mark, another runner passed me by on the right side. I immediately thought, "Oh no! Someone is passing me. I have got to pick up my pace." And so I did. I picked up my pace, passed them, and then created enough distance that I could settle back into the pace that was prescribed for the 18 mile run. Within a few minutes, this same runner passed me by again and I again thought, "Oh no!" and picked up my pace, passing them once again. At the next corner, this runner turned left and I turned right according to my mapped out course, glad to no longer feel the pressure of another runner and relieved to settle back into my pace. By mile 15, I had hit "the wall." The wall is when you have used up all of your glycogen stores and have no more available energy in your body to move forward. I had heard of it but had never hit it until now. I literally stopped. It took every bit of mental and physical effort I could summon to walk the rest of my course and make it back home. I know why it happened—the lack of glycogen. But why? Simply put, I compared my race to somebody else's that day. I learned a valuable lesson, and from then on, when another runner passes by, I simply tell myself, "I don't know what their race is today. I know what mine is. Stick to it!"

This lesson has served me well in running as well as in life. We often compare where we are in life with where others are. Remember, we do not know their life race- where they've been and where they are going- and if we try to run their race instead of ours, we will most certainly hit "the wall." Focus on your race, and you will be the winner in your life.

When in your life have you compared your situation to somebody else's? How could you be grateful for the race you are in? How would that change the outcome?

Monday

G _____

L _____

A _____

D _____

S _____

Tuesday

G _____

L _____

A _____

D _____

S _____

Wednesday

G _____

L _____

A _____

D _____

S _____

Thursday

G _____

L _____

A _____

D _____

S _____

Friday

G _____

L _____

A _____

D _____

S _____

Saturday

G _____

L _____

A _____

D _____

S _____

Sunday

G _____

L _____

A _____

D _____

S _____

"Top GLADS" for this week:

G _____

L _____

A _____

D _____

S _____

Aware:

Use the space below to review your week nonjudgmentally. What did you notice in your gratitude practice? Where did you do great? Where can you improve? What were the obstacles? What were the "wins"?

Assess:

Score yourself in each area below on a 1-10 scale, with 10 being "top notch!"

Physical	Emotional	Relational	Overall
_____	_____	_____	_____

Goals or ideas for improving in any of these areas:

Affirm:

Use the space below to positively acknowledge and affirm anything about yourself or your efforts from this past week:

Week Fifteen
Loss

Loss is nothing else but change, and change is nature's delight.

-Marcus Aurelius

Our first reaction to losing something tends to be negative. We get angry, grieve, and ask, "Why me? Why did this happen? Why now?" Marcus Aurelius, the Philosopher and the last of the Roman rulers known as the Five Good Emperors, offers a shift in our paradigm for loss. Looking at nature, we see leaves losing their green color in autumn, but they are not just losing their greenness; they are changing color. People love to take long drives to delight in the changing leaves of fall. Then, of course, the trees lose their leaves entirely, and there is barrenness. This barrenness makes room for the blossoms of spring. Loss is change. Where we once had something, we no longer do; there is now a space. Sometimes that space feels barren, like the winter branches on the trees, but that barrenness is there to allow something different and beautiful to come along, like the blossoms of spring. Can you identify a loss and view it with gratitude or delight for what it might mean?

Week Fifteen
GLADS

Monday

G _____

L _____

A _____

D _____

S _____

Tuesday

G _____

L _____

A _____

D _____

S _____

Wednesday

G _____

L _____

A _____

D _____

S _____

Thursday

G _____

L _____

A _____

D _____

S _____

Friday

G _____

L _____

A _____

D _____

S _____

Saturday

G _____

L _____

A _____

D _____

S _____

Sunday

G _____

L _____

A _____

D _____

S _____

"Top GLADS" for this week:

G _____

L _____

A _____

D _____

S _____

Aware:

Use the space below to review your week nonjudgmentally. What did you notice in your gratitude practice? Where did you do great? Where can you improve? What were the obstacles? What were the "wins"?

Assess:

Score yourself in each area below on a 1-10 scale, with 10 being "top notch!"

Physical	Emotional	Relational	Overall
_____	_____	_____	_____

Goals or ideas for improving in any of these areas:

Affirm:

Use the space below to positively acknowledge and affirm anything about yourself or your efforts from this past week:

Week Sixteen

Fears

Too many of us are not living our dreams because we are living our fears.

-Les Brown

One of my favorite movies is Pretty Woman with Richard Gere and Julia Roberts. As the movie ends, there is a scene with a man walking down Hollywood Boulevard calling out to everyone, "What's your dream? Everybody comes here; this is Hollywood, the land of dreams...." We don't need to travel to Hollywood for our dreams to become a reality, but we do need to step outside of our self-limiting comfort zone of fear and doubt and go straight into the land of our fears. It is the only way to discover if those fears have merit. My guess is that they don't; if they do, it is not as bad as your mind has made it out to be.

When I was in early elementary school, my mother signed my older brother and me up for summer swimming lessons. I was two years younger than the other students, but it made it easier for my mother to have us both in the same class. Not to be outdone by the older kids, I did great with learning the basics of swimming: deadman's float, treading water, backstroke, and front crawl. Our final test for passing swim class was jumping off the high dive into the 12 feet of water at the "deep end" and swimming to the pool's edge. I remember climbing the ladder, walking to the end of the diving board, and staring down into the water below me. I stared and stared. The longer I stared, the deeper the water and the higher the platform seemed. I felt fear rising inside of me. I could not do it. I was embarrassed to have to turn around and back down the ladder, but it was easier at that point than jumping off the board and into the water.

I had one more week to accomplish this feat to pass the swim class. The following week came, and my first time up the ladder and out to the edge of the diving board played out just as it had the week prior. I was afraid. I turned and climbed back down the ladder. I watched as one classmate after another completed the jump and the swim to the edge. I noticed something as I watched from the pool deck. I noticed they did not stare down into the water when they were at the edge of the diving board. They walked to the edge, glanced down, and then jumped. Finally, everyone but me had jumped. I decided to give it another try; this time, I would not stare down into the water. This time, I would only think of my desire to pass the class. I climbed up the ladder and walked to the edge of the board; for just a second, I glanced down at the 12 feet of water below me, then I closed my eyes, plugged my nose, and jumped. I could feel my heart beat fast, and then I splashed into the water, and down I went. My heart raced more quickly as I scrambled to bring myself to the water's surface, where I could finally breathe. The water had not swallowed me up as I feared. I breathed a mix of relief and pride as I swam my way over to the edge of the pool and climbed out. I had done it! Fear is nothing more than False Evidence Appearing Real. The water was not going to swallow me up. The water did not become deeper, nor did the diving board become higher. My fear created those things, I chose to believe them as accurate, and as long as I thought it, it was real to me.

The only way you can discover if your doubts are real is to test them out. You can find out for yourself. As the saying goes, "Feel the fear and do it anyway!" When was the last time you took time to think about what you wanted in your personal and professional life? What fears are keeping you from living your dreams? Is it a case of False Evidence Appearing Real?

Week Sixteen
GLADS

Monday

G _____

L _____

A _____

D _____

S _____

Tuesday

G _____

L _____

A _____

D _____

S _____

Wednesday

G _____

L _____

A _____

D _____

S _____

Thursday

G _____

L _____

A _____

D _____

S _____

Friday

G _____

L _____

A _____

D _____

S _____

Saturday

G _____

L _____

A _____

D _____

S _____

Week Sixteen
GLADS

Sunday

G _____

L _____

A _____

D _____

S _____

"Top GLADS" for this week:

G _____

L _____

A _____

D _____

S _____

Aware:

Use the space below to review your week nonjudgmentally. What did you notice in your gratitude practice? Where did you do great? Where can you improve? What were the obstacles? What were the "wins"?

Assess:

Score yourself in each area below on a 1-10 scale, with 10 being "top notch!"

Physical	Emotional	Relational	Overall
_____	_____	_____	_____

Goals or ideas for improving in any of these areas:

Affirm:

Use the space below to positively acknowledge and affirm anything about yourself or your efforts from this past week:

Week Seventeen

Tolerance

In the practice of tolerance, one's enemy is the best teacher.

-Dalai Lama

In the spring of 2020, the world was introduced to its newest enemy—COVID-19. This coronavirus was like no other virus and soon became a worldwide pandemic. During the pandemic, people started hoarding toilet paper, hand sanitizer, disinfectant wipes/sprays, surgical masks, latex gloves, eggs, and even yeast. Some of these items made sense to have on hand, given the nature of the virus, and other items (e.g., toilet paper) made no sense at all. People were panicked. There had not been anything like this in over a century, and we were not prepared. Slowly, people's lives became increasingly restricted until finally only essential workers could go to work, parks and beaches were closed, schools were closed, and unless a store sold items deemed essential, stores were closed. If someone needed to get groceries, a mask covering the nose and mouth was required. The virus had attacked us and was our number one enemy. People were tolerating this enemy while medical experts desperately searched for a weapon to use against this coronavirus. And then, as days of quarantine turned into weeks, something happened. This enemy, COVID-19, began to teach those of us who were open to learning. This enemy taught us how to tune in to each other and ourselves. In the absence of our usual go-to's, people began to connect with their families. Families were doing board games and jigsaw puzzles. Families were cooking and having meals together. People were walking and riding bicycles. People were learning new hobbies such as drawing, painting, and crocheting. Yards were being cared for, and houses were cleaned and organized, and as the enemy plundered on, we became quiet and connected with each other and ourselves. People got creative in how to connect while staying physically distant, and for the first time in a long time, people felt connected. I am grateful for my gratitude practice that allowed me to see COVID-19 as a teacher and to be grateful for the lessons that have come out of this pandemic. I am hopeful that these lessons will not be forgotten. Whatever enemy you are currently facing, how can it become your teacher?

Week Seventeen
GLADS

Monday

G _____

L _____

A _____

D _____

S _____

Tuesday

G _____

L _____

A _____

D _____

S _____

GLADS

Wednesday

G _____

L _____

A _____

D _____

S _____

Thursday

G _____

L _____

A _____

D _____

S _____

Week Seventeen
GLADS

Friday

G _____

L _____

A _____

D _____

S _____

Saturday

G _____

L _____

A _____

D _____

S _____

Sunday

G _____

L _____

A _____

D _____

S _____

"Top GLADS" for this week:

G _____

L _____

A _____

D _____

S _____

Aware:

Use the space below to review your week nonjudgmentally. What did you notice in your gratitude practice? Where did you do great? Where can you improve? What were the obstacles? What were the "wins"?

Assess:

Score yourself in each area below on a 1-10 scale, with 10 being "top notch!"

Physical	Emotional	Relational	Overall
_____	_____	_____	_____

Goals or ideas for improving in any of these areas:

Affirm:

Use the space below to positively acknowledge and affirm anything about yourself or your efforts from this past week:

Week Eighteen

Disappointment

Disappointments are inevitable; discouragement is a choice.

-Charles F. Stanley

Disappointment is the emotion we experience when something we hoped for or expected does not come to pass. We have all experienced this emotion many times. Sometimes it is disappointment at not getting an "A" on a test you studied hard for or a job or promotion that went to someone else. Other times, it is disappointment in our relationships and how we thought someone would respond to us. Disappointments are the ups and downs of life. They are inevitable and even necessary. They are necessary because, without disappointment, we could not experience joy. While disappointment is an emotion specific to an event, discouragement, on the other hand, is a generalized loss of enthusiasm to the point of gloom and despair.

Perhaps the most poignant examples of disappointment and discouragement can be drawn from A.A. Milne's wonderful characters who reside in the Hundred Acre Wood. Tigger is known for his exuberance in nearly all situations but there are times when he does experience disappointment. Tigger takes on the red balloon in one story, thinking it a foe. After a series of pounces and tumbles, Tigger states, "This isn't working out the way I was hoping." He then considers making the balloon his sidekick in being the hero and defender of the Hundred Acre Wood. Tigger experienced disappointment but reframed the situation such that he did not experience discouragement.

Contrast this to Eeyore, who is undoubtedly characterized by his gloomy pessimism. In the story In which Eeyore Loses a Tail and Pooh finds one, Pooh greets Eeyore with, "Lovely day, isn't it?" Eeyore replies, "If it is a good morning, which I doubt." Eventually, Pooh finds Eeyore's tail, and Christopher Robin pins it on Eeyore, asking, "There now. Did I get your tail back on properly, Eeyore?" Eeyore replies, "No matter. Most likely lose it again anyway." For whatever reason, Eeyore has chosen to let disappointments become a discouragement.

Are you a Tigger or an Eeyore? Perhaps you have had so many disappointments in life that it is seemingly impossible and even scary to feel optimistic. If this is the case, take a moment to consider the pros and cons of discouragement. Yes, there are pros to discouragement. Discouragement may have protected you from disappointment, but it has also denied you hope and joy. If you have become discouraged in life, daily gratitude will bring you hope and encouragement.

Week Eighteen
GLADS

Monday

G _____

L _____

A _____

D _____

S _____

Tuesday

G _____

L _____

A _____

D _____

S _____

Wednesday

G _____

L _____

A _____

D _____

S _____

Thursday

G _____

L _____

A _____

D _____

S _____

GLADS

Friday

G _____

L _____

A _____

D _____

S _____

Saturday

G _____

L _____

A _____

D _____

S _____

Sunday

G _____

L _____

A _____

D _____

S _____

 ## "Top GLADS" for this week:

G _____

L _____

A _____

D _____

S _____

Aware:

Use the space below to review your week nonjudgmentally. What did you notice in your gratitude practice? Where did you do great? Where can you improve? What were the obstacles? What were the "wins"?

Assess:

Score yourself in each area below on a 1-10 scale, with 10 being "top notch!"

Physical	Emotional	Relational	Overall
_____	_____	_____	_____

Goals or ideas for improving in any of these areas:

Affirm:

Use the space below to positively acknowledge and affirm anything about yourself or your efforts from this past week:

Week Nineteen

Forgiveness

Inner peace can be reached only when we practice forgiveness. Forgiveness is letting go of the past, and is, therefore the means for correcting our misperceptions.

-Gerald Jamposky

Forgiveness is, perhaps, one of the most difficult acts of love and kindness, especially when we have been deeply wounded by someone. A quick search of the internet will reveal thousands of quotes and hundreds of books on forgiveness. Clearly, forgiveness is important, so why do so many of us hold onto grudges and unforgiveness? It may be because we do not truly understand what forgiveness is and what forgiveness is not.

I once heard a story about a husband and wife. The wife was going away with her girlfriends for a weekend girl's trip. As she drove off, her husband decided he would finally clean out the garage she had been asking him to do for several months, thinking this would be a wonderful surprise for her upon her return from the girl's trip. He promptly went about the task, clearing out old tools, half-used paint, and other junk and boxes that had accumulated over the years. Finally, on Sunday afternoon, the garage was clean, neat, and organized. He smiled with pride and anticipation at how pleased his wife would be when she could finally park her car in the garage.

The wife came home, excited to share the details of her girl's trip. He listened, happy to hear she had a good time and eager to show her the garage. When she finished sharing about her trip, he told her he had something he wanted to show her. He took her hand, led her out to the garage, and turned on the light. As he anticipated, she was thrilled!

A few weeks later, the wife was getting ready for her upcoming high school reunion and wanted to look through her yearbook. She went out to the garage in search of the box that contained her high school memorabilia. As you might have guessed, it was gone. Her husband had mistakenly thrown it out with other boxes when he was cleaning the garage. She was greatly saddened as these are things that cannot be replaced. Her husband promptly and profusely apologized. He felt terrible about this mistake. He contacted her former high school to attempt to replace the yearbook, which he was able to do, but the rest of her high school things were gone forever. She forgave her husband for this mistake. But whenever she thinks about high school, she feels a twinge of sadness at the loss of her memorabilia. She cannot forget that these things are now gone, but she does not feel angry towards her spouse for his mistake.

Forgiveness is not forgetting. Forgiveness is choosing to let go of the need to get even. It is freeing ourselves from the burden of negative thoughts and feelings about a situation that we have no power to change, and in so doing, we change our present and our future for the better.

Monday

G _____

L _____

A _____

D _____

S _____

Tuesday

G _____

L _____

A _____

D _____

S _____

Wednesday

G _____

L _____

A _____

D _____

S _____

Thursday

G _____

L _____

A _____

D _____

S _____

Friday

G _____

L _____

A _____

D _____

S _____

Saturday

G _____

L _____

A _____

D _____

S _____

Week Ninteen
GLADS

Sunday

G _____

L _____

A _____

D _____

S _____

 "Top GLADS" for this week:

G _____

L _____

A _____

D _____

S _____

Aware:

Use the space below to review your week nonjudgmentally. What did you notice in your gratitude practice? Where did you do great? Where can you improve? What were the obstacles? What were the "wins"?

Assess:

Score yourself in each area below on a 1-10 scale, with 10 being "top notch!"

Physical	Emotional	Relational	Overall

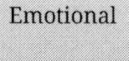 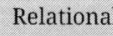

Goals or ideas for improving in any of these areas:

Affirm:

Use the space below to positively acknowledge and affirm anything about yourself or your efforts from this past week:

Week Twenty
Self-Care

Rest and self-care are so important. When you take time to replenish your spirit, it allows you to serve others from the overflow. You cannot serve from an empty vessel.

-Eleanor Brown

The Bike Lesson, a story from The Berenstain Bears children's literature series, tells the story of Papa Bear bringing home a shiny, new bike for Brother Bear. Papa Bear takes Brother Bear out for a bike lesson before allowing Brother Bear to ride the bike. The story consists of a number of errors Papa Bear makes, such as riding on the wrong side of the street. Each time he makes an error, Papa Bear tells Brother Bear, "That is what you should not do. Now let that be a lesson to you." Just as Brother Bear learned how to properly ride a bike by observing what not to do, I learned self-care by observing my mother. My mother had eight children, and as is if taking care of eight children was not enough, she always held positions in her church. She did not know how to say "no" effectively, and she put everybody ahead of herself. This took its toll on her both physically and emotionally. While I fully believe she wanted nothing more than to be a wonderful, loving mother, she simply did not have the energy stores to carry out this desire effectively. Her vessel was empty.

When I became a mother, I took to heart what I had observed. I, too, wanted to be the best mom I could be, which meant taking care of myself first. Self-care is not selfishness. It is quite the opposite. It is making sure you are fully replenished so that you can give fully—whether it is at home, in your career, or with friends. If you are operating at 50 percent, then you can only give 50 percent at best. Your family, friends, career, etc., deserve 100 percent, don't they? So what can you do to make sure you are replenishing your spirit today and every day?

GLADS

Monday

G _____

L _____

A _____

D _____

S _____

Tuesday

G _____

L _____

A _____

D _____

S _____

Wednesday

G _____

L _____

A _____

D _____

S _____

Thursday

G _____

L _____

A _____

D _____

S _____

Friday

G _____

L _____

A _____

D _____

S _____

Saturday

G _____

L _____

A _____

D _____

S _____

Week Twenty
GLADS

Sunday

G _____

L _____

A _____

D _____

S _____

"Top GLADS" for this week:

G _____

L _____

A _____

D _____

S _____

Aware:

Use the space below to review your week nonjudgmentally. What did you notice in your gratitude practice? Where did you do great? Where can you improve? What were the obstacles? What were the "wins"?

Assess:

Score yourself in each area below on a 1-10 scale, with 10 being "top notch!"

Physical	Emotional	Relational	Overall
_____	_____	_____	_____

Goals or ideas for improving in any of these areas:

Affirm:

Use the space below to positively acknowledge and affirm anything about yourself or your efforts from this past week:

Week Twenty-One

Miracles

There are only two ways to live your life. One is as though nothing is a miracle. The other is as though everything is a miracle.

-Albert Einstein

Thanks to pranks played on me by my brothers when I was a young girl, I have never liked spiders. Further, as a runner, there is nothing more annoying than running face first into a spider web and then trying to get the sticky, fine threads of the web off your face without messing up your running pace. Needless to say, spiders and their webs have just been yucky to me until one particular day when my view of spiders and webs was forever changed.

When my daughter was ten years old, we were taking a walk along a paved, quiet, tree-lined path in the suburbs. She spotted a spider web, a rather large, intricate spider web, which had been spun overnight. As she pointed it out to me, she said, "Momma, isn't it cool how a spider just knows how to spin a web?". Through the eyes of a child, I could now see this "yucky" thing as a miracle. How would your day be different if you viewed everything today as though it were a miracle?

Monday

G _____

L _____

A _____

D _____

S _____

Tuesday

G _____

L _____

A _____

D _____

S _____

Wednesday

G _____

L _____

A _____

D _____

S _____

Thursday

G _____

L _____

A _____

D _____

S _____

GLADS

Friday

G _____

L _____

A _____

D _____

S _____

Saturday

G _____

L _____

A _____

D _____

S _____

Week Twenty-One
GLADS

Sunday

G _____

L _____

A _____

D _____

S _____

"Top GLADS" for this week:

G _____

L _____

A _____

D _____

S _____

Aware:

Use the space below to review your week nonjudgmentally. What did you notice in your gratitude practice? Where did you do great? Where can you improve? What were the obstacles? What were the "wins"?

Assess:

Score yourself in each area below on a 1-10 scale, with 10 being "top notch!"

Physical	Emotional	Relational	Overall
_____	_____	_____	_____

Goals or ideas for improving in any of these areas:

Affirm:

Use the space below to positively acknowledge and affirm anything about yourself or your efforts from this past week:

Week Twenty-Two

Clutter

To give without any reward or any notice has a special quality of its own.

-Anne Morrow Lindbergh

I am honored to have had the opportunity to serve our country as a member of the United States Air Force. At one particular Air Force base, I became close with a certain squadron commander. This commander exhibited consistently strong leadership skills that led to a significantly positive change in his squadron's morale. The composition of this squadron was quite diverse, ranging from officers with engineering degrees to firefighters to enlisted members with no college degrees who were charged with construction and grounds maintenance. Historically, the latter group was often overlooked when it came to awards time. They did the dirty work that no one noticed unless it was not done. This particular commander, however, noticed this gap and created a special award that could recognize the work these service members performed faithfully every day. He aptly named this award the "Knuckle Buster." He once stated that this award had done more to boost the morale of his Airmen than anything else. This commander would beam every time the Knuckle Buster award was mentioned.

After three years of serving as the squadron commander, he was going to be transferred to another base. In pondering a going away gift for his Change of Command ceremony, I knew what would be the best gift. I spoke with the commander's First Sergeant and arranged for an engraved Knuckle Buster award to be presented to the commander at the ceremony. It was perfect. When his First Sergeant presented him with the Knuckle Buster, the commander could not help but to break military decorum and allow the joy to spread across his face and into a laugh. He never knew I had arranged it, and I have never told him. It is my own special secret (now shared with you as anonymously as possible) that always makes me feel warm inside when I reflect back on it.

Perhaps you can spend some time today planning something you can do for someone this week without ever letting them know it was you.

Week Twenty-Two
GLADS

Monday

G _____

L _____

A _____

D _____

S _____

Tuesday

G _____

L _____

A _____

D _____

S _____

Wednesday

G _____

L _____

A _____

D _____

S _____

Thursday

G _____

L _____

A _____

D _____

S _____

Friday

G _____

L _____

A _____

D _____

S _____

Saturday

G _____

L _____

A _____

D _____

S _____

Sunday

G _____

L _____

A _____

D _____

S _____

"Top GLADS" for this week:

G _____

L _____

A _____

D _____

S _____

Aware:

Use the space below to review your week nonjudgmentally. What did you notice in your gratitude practice? Where did you do great? Where can you improve? What were the obstacles? What were the "wins"?

Assess:

Score yourself in each area below on a 1-10 scale, with 10 being "top notch!"

Physical	Emotional	Relational	Overall
_____	_____	_____	_____

Goals or ideas for improving in any of these areas:

Affirm:

Use the space below to positively acknowledge and affirm anything about yourself or your efforts from this past week:

Week Twenty-Three

Kindness

To be yourself in a world that is constantly trying to make you something else is the greatest accomplishment.

--Ralph Waldo Emerson

Compare our 21st-century world to the 19th-century world when Emerson wrote about the challenge of being your authentic self. How much more of a struggle this is for us today, with social media constantly persuading us of how we should look, think, and act in order to be liked and accepted. In order to be ourselves, we need to quiet the world around us and simply be with ourselves.

An interesting exercise is to sit down with a stack of various magazines and begin to cut out whatever appeals to you without questioning why it appeals to you. You can cut out scenery, home décor, activities, and even words. I recommend doing this for an hour or two each week for a couple of weeks. Simply cut out what appeals to you and place them into a manila envelope. When you have a pretty good collection of cut-outs, you can then begin to make a collage with them. Look at each cut-out one at a time, considering if it truly reflects you on the inside or if it is something that is not part of the real you but rather a reflection of the outside world's influence on you and whom you think you should be. Glue the "authentic you" cut-outs on one side of the poster board and the "world-influenced" cut-outs on the other side. When you are finished, meditate on how you feel when you look at one side of the collage versus the other side. What would you need to do to be more authentically you? Not only is being yourself the greatest accomplishment, but it is also the greatest peace you can have.

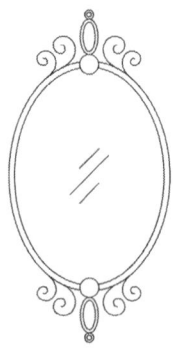

Monday

G _____

L _____

A _____

D _____

S _____

Tuesday

G _____

L _____

A _____

D _____

S _____

Wednesday

G _____

L _____

A _____

D _____

S _____

Thursday

G _____

L _____

A _____

D _____

S _____

Week Twenty-Three
GLADS

Friday

G _____

L _____

A _____

D _____

S _____

Saturday

G _____

L _____

A _____

D _____

S _____

Week Twenty-Three
GLADS

Sunday

G _____

L _____

A _____

D _____

S _____

"Top GLADS" for this week:

G _____

L _____

A _____

D _____

S _____

Aware:

Use the space below to review your week nonjudgmentally. What did you notice in your gratitude practice? Where did you do great? Where can you improve? What were the obstacles? What were the "wins"?

Assess:

Score yourself in each area below on a 1-10 scale, with 10 being "top notch!"

Physical	Emotional	Relational	Overall
_____	_____	_____	_____

Goals or ideas for improving in any of these areas:

Affirm:

Use the space below to positively acknowledge and affirm anything about yourself or your efforts from this past week:

Week Twenty-Four
Inner Child

Forget not that the earth delights to feel your bare feet and the winds long to play with your hair.

-Khalil Gribran

When was the last time you romped around barefoot or let the wind just dance through your hair without worrying about how you looked? Sadly, in adulthood, we begin to take life all too seriously, and we lose touch with our inner child. The inner child loves to be playful, carefree, and just live in the moment. I fondly recall watching my daughter as she joyously jumped into every puddle of rain she could find. She was thrilled with how much she could make the water splash out of the puddle. She did not care about her pants being wet or her feet being soaked. It was just plain and simple fun.

I learned a lot about my inner child by being a parent. I knew I had not had the opportunity to have much of a childhood, and being a parent allowed me to not only see what childhood looked like, but it also called my inner child to come out and play. I have learned that being an adult does not mean all work and no play. Rather, being a healthy adult means finding the balance between seriousness and playfulness. This week, allow your inner child to come out to play. Walk barefoot on the lawn, try that cartwheel, or blow some bubbles. Consider things you enjoyed as a child. Maybe you put together model cars, or you liked to color, or you loved board games. Begin to add these things back into your life and experience the joy of childhood again or maybe for the first time.

Monday

G _____

L _____

A _____

D _____

S _____

Tuesday

G _____

L _____

A _____

D _____

S _____

Wednesday

G _____

L _____

A _____

D _____

S _____

Thursday

G _____

L _____

A _____

D _____

S _____

Friday

G _____

L _____

A _____

D _____

S _____

Saturday

G _____

L _____

A _____

D _____

S _____

Sunday

G _____

L _____

A _____

D _____

S _____

"Top GLADS" for this week:

G _____

L _____

A _____

D _____

S _____

Aware:

Use the space below to review your week nonjudgmentally. What did you notice in your gratitude practice? Where did you do great? Where can you improve? What were the obstacles? What were the "wins"?

Assess:

Score yourself in each area below on a 1-10 scale, with 10 being "top notch!"

Physical	Emotional	Relational	Overall
_____	_____	_____	_____

Goals or ideas for improving in any of these areas:

Affirm:

Use the space below to positively acknowledge and affirm anything about yourself or your efforts from this past week:

Week Twenty-Five
Showing Love

They do not love that do not show love.

-William Shakespeare

This morning was a hurried morning for me. I had fallen behind schedule before I even got out of bed. I set about my day in a rush to make up for lost time, and by the time I left the house, I had almost caught up on my morning routine. As I was driving to work, I noticed an odd feeling, like something was missing. I checked that I had my cell phone, iPad, and other necessary items for the day. I had them all. And then it hit me. In my rush to accomplish all of the "important" things, I failed to do the most important thing. I did not give my husband a loving goodbye. I had made a hurried statement of "Love you, have a good day," as I had rushed out the door.

How often do we feel love and yet not show love? I am reminded of a USAF major that came to see me for therapy regarding his marriage. Several weeks into therapy, it appeared he was understanding how he had put his marriage on autopilot and needed to put more effort into showing his wife he loved her. He came into therapy one afternoon and enthusiastically shared that he had been in the local grocery store, saw a bouquet of flowers at the checkout stand, and thought, "My wife would love those flowers." I was happy that he had been able to step outside of his busy head to consider his wife. Never one to make assumptions, I then asked him if he had bought them for her and what her reaction was. My excitement at this new development was quickly squashed as he told me that he didn't buy them, but he did think about it. We may feel the love in our hearts, but if we do not put that feeling into action, it is as if it does not exist. The major bought the flowers the next time.

After realizing what was "missing," once I arrived at work, I reached out and told my husband I loved him. What love do you have in your heart that you need to put into action this week?

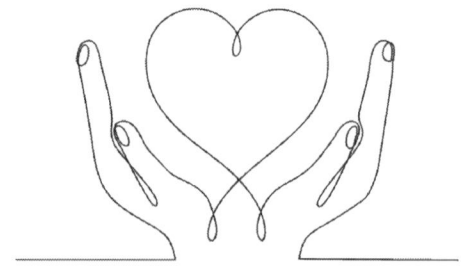

Monday

G _____

L _____

A _____

D _____

S _____

Tuesday

G _____

L _____

A _____

D _____

S _____

Wednesday

G _____

L _____

A _____

D _____

S _____

Thursday

G _____

L _____

A _____

D _____

S _____

Friday

G _____

L _____

A _____

D _____

S _____

Saturday

G _____

L _____

A _____

D _____

S _____

Sunday

G _____

L _____

A _____

D _____

S _____

"Top GLADS" for this week:

G _____

L _____

A _____

D _____

S _____

Aware:

Use the space below to review your week nonjudgmentally. What did you notice in your gratitude practice? Where did you do great? Where can you improve? What were the obstacles? What were the "wins"?

Assess:

Score yourself in each area below on a 1-10 scale, with 10 being "top notch!"

Physical	Emotional	Relational	Overall

Goals or ideas for improving in any of these areas:

Affirm:

Use the space below to positively acknowledge and affirm anything about yourself or your efforts from this past week:

Week Twenty-Six
Peace

Peace comes from within. Do not seek it without.

-Buddha

There is a story of a king who offered a prize to the artist who painted the best picture of peace. Many artists submitted their paintings of peace, and after carefully studying all of the entries, the king finally had it narrowed down to two paintings. One was a painting of a calm lake. The lake perfectly reflected the majestic mountains all around it. Above the lake was a blue sky sprinkled with fluffy white clouds. To all who saw this painting, this was the perfect picture of peace.

The other painting was of rugged, bare mountains. Above these mountains was an angry sky from which rain fell and lightning flashed. Down the side of the mountain was a raging waterfall. By all who saw this painting, it certainly did not look peaceful. But when the king looked closely at the second painting, he saw behind the waterfall a tiny bush growing in a crack in the rock. In the bush, a mother bird had built her nest. There, in the midst of the rush of angry water, sat the mother bird on her nest in perfect peace.

To the surprise of all, the king chose this second painting to be the winner. The king explained, "Peace does not mean to be in a place where there is no noise, trouble, or hard work. Peace means to be in the midst of all those things and still be calm in your heart."

Inner peace is the state of being mentally and spiritually at peace regardless of our circumstances. If we think we will find peace when X happens or when Y changes, we will never be at peace. Accepting where we are at any given moment and looking for how we can grow or find meaning in our personal storms is the pathway to peace.

What are you learning from your current circumstances? Can you be grateful for the challenges you are experiencing?

Week Twenty-Six
GLADS

Monday

G _____

L _____

A _____

D _____

S _____

Tuesday

G _____

L _____

A _____

D _____

S _____

Wednesday

G _____

L _____

A _____

D _____

S _____

Thursday

G _____

L _____

A _____

D _____

S _____

Friday

G _____

L _____

A _____

D _____

S _____

Saturday

G _____

L _____

A _____

D _____

S _____

Sunday

G _____

L _____

A _____

D _____

S _____

"Top GLADS" for this week:

G _____

L _____

A _____

D _____

S _____

Aware:

Use the space below to review your week nonjudgmentally. What did you notice in your gratitude practice? Where did you do great? Where can you improve? What were the obstacles? What were the "wins"?

Assess:

Score yourself in each area below on a 1-10 scale, with 10 being "top notch!"

Physical	Emotional	Relational	Overall
_____	_____	_____	_____

Goals or ideas for improving in any of these areas:

Affirm:

Use the space below to positively acknowledge and affirm anything about yourself or your efforts from this past week:

Week Twenty-Seven
Expectations

My happiness grows in direct proportion to my acceptance and in inverse proportion to my expectations.

-Michael J. Fox

Michael J. Fox won the hearts of many in his acting roles in the hit TV series Family Ties and the blockbuster movie series Back to the Future, to name just a few. By all accounts, he was a success, but in 1991 he was diagnosed with Parkinson's disease and soon turned to alcohol to cope. To Michael J Fox and to others, it seemed the best of life for him was over. But after a year of drinking, he turned to therapy to help him cope in a healthier way and to accept his diagnosis. He stated in an interview, "Acceptance is not resignation; it means understanding that something is what it is and that there's got to be a way through it."

Michael J Fox continues to act, to be a father, to be a husband, and in 2000 he and his wife founded the Michael J Fox Foundation for Parkinson's research. This foundation has raised nearly $1 billion for research, and Michael J Fox remains hopeful that through this, researchers will be able to predict and stop the disease.

We all have expectations about life and relationships. Expectations are dangerous. If things turn out as expected, our reaction is neutral. If, however, things do not turn out as expected, our reaction is negative. Happiness comes by way of accepting what is. When we accept, we let go of the "why's, if only, and the how come's." Letting go of these futile questions allows us to see what we have and figure out how to make meaning out of what is. What can you accept this week in order to grow your happiness?

Week Twenty-Seven
GLADS

Monday

G _____

L _____

A _____

D _____

S _____

Tuesday

G _____

L _____

A _____

D _____

S _____

GLADS

Wednesday

G _____

L _____

A _____

D _____

S _____

Thursday

G _____

L _____

A _____

D _____

S _____

Week Twenty-Seven
GLADS

Friday

G _____

L _____

A _____

D _____

S _____

Saturday

G _____

L _____

A _____

D _____

S _____

Sunday

G _____

L _____

A _____

D _____

S _____

"Top GLADS" for this week:

G _____

L _____

A _____

D _____

S _____

Aware:

Use the space below to review your week nonjudgmentally. What did you notice in your gratitude practice? Where did you do great? Where can you improve? What were the obstacles? What were the "wins"?

Assess:

Score yourself in each area below on a 1-10 scale, with 10 being "top notch!"

Physical	Emotional	Relational	Overall
_____	_____	_____	_____

Goals or ideas for improving in any of these areas:

Affirm:

Use the space below to positively acknowledge and affirm anything about yourself or your efforts from this past week:

Week Twenty-Eight

Attitude

Your attitude, not your aptitude, will determine your altitude.

-Zig Zigler

At five years of age, my son was diagnosed with a nonverbal learning disability and a language processing disability. He struggled with organization, writing with a pencil, cutting with scissors, and had a slight lisp in his speech. He could not keep up with conversations and had difficulty looking at people when they spoke because the nonverbal information interfered with his ability to track the verbal information. It took him longer to process what had been said and then even longer to formulate a response. This created a great deal of difficulty in his academic and social life. Many years later, he was diagnosed as being on the autism spectrum. By all accounts, my son's aptitude would be considered inferior, and the odds of him succeeding in school would be low.

In contrast to his predicted aptitude, my son has earned an associate's degree and has completed multiple certifications in the computer science and information systems field. Presently, he works a full-time job, has been promoted to supervisor, and has purchased his own car. He is a runner and an avid reader of books. He has beaten the odds. How? Through his attitude. He understood things would take longer for him and would be difficult for him. Not only did he accept these challenges, but he worked with them. He did not use them as a reason to quit but as a reason to work harder. My son would be at the dining room table for hours working on homework that I knew other children would have finished in 45 minutes. He just kept working. He didn't give up. His attitude of perseverance continues to extend his altitude, and I could not be more proud of him. He took a challenge and turned it into a character strength.

Is your attitude toward certain things preventing you from reaching a higher altitude? We cannot change things that have happened, but we can change our attitude toward those things. This week, identify one thing you can develop a more positive attitude towards, and then feel yourself soar to a higher height.

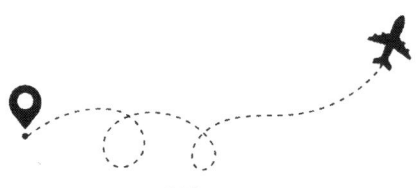

Monday

G _____

L _____

A _____

D _____

S _____

Tuesday

G _____

L _____

A _____

D _____

S _____

Wednesday

G _____

L _____

A _____

D _____

S _____

Thursday

G _____

L _____

A _____

D _____

S _____

Friday

G _____

L _____

A _____

D _____

S _____

Saturday

G _____

L _____

A _____

D _____

S _____

Sunday

G _____

L _____

A _____

D _____

S _____

"Top GLADS" for this week:

G _____

L _____

A _____

D _____

S _____

Aware:

Use the space below to review your week nonjudgmentally. What did you notice in your gratitude practice? Where did you do great? Where can you improve? What were the obstacles? What were the "wins"?

Assess:

Score yourself in each area below on a 1-10 scale, with 10 being "top notch!"

Physical	Emotional	Relational	Overall
_____	_____	_____	_____

Goals or ideas for improving in any of these areas:

Affirm:

Use the space below to positively acknowledge and affirm anything about yourself or your efforts from this past week:

Week Twenty-Nine

Wants

What I want is what I've not got, and what I need is all around me.

-Dave Matthews

How many times have you said or heard others say, "I will be happy when..." It seems we are always looking for the next thing that will fulfill us, whether it is losing another five pounds, getting married, having a baby, getting a new car, or getting that promotion. With our eyes so focused on that next thing, we are unable to rest in the joy of what we do have.

I am a Dave Matthews fan, and I had heard the song lyric "What I want is what I've not got and what I need is all around me" so many times, but it never stood out to me until one particular morning a few years ago. I was out on my morning run, and as I often do on my runs, I was processing where I was in life and where I wanted to be. I was thinking through my career, my relationship, and my finances and admittedly had begun thinking, "I can't wait until...then..." I was thinking that I would be happier when certain things happened. And then I heard, "What I want is what I've not got, and what I need is all around me." Those words literally stopped me in my tracks. I hit the back button and listened to that line again, and this time, I looked around me and realized I truly had everything I needed. I live in a beautiful location with a climate that is perfect for me. My loved ones are healthy and safe. I get to earn a living doing my passion. I have a car, a home, and food to eat. I have hobbies. I have my health. I was flooded by all of the things that I have, and I realized how wanting other things was robbing me of fully experiencing joy each and every day.

Sure, there are things that we all want. There is nothing wrong with wanting, for it motivates action. The problem arises when we focus on our wants and believe our happiness will come when we finally have all of those things we want. Happiness grows from gratitude, gratitude for all we currently have, which truly is all that we really need.

Monday

G _____

L _____

A _____

D _____

S _____

Tuesday

G _____

L _____

A _____

D _____

S _____

Week Twenty-Nine
GLADS

Wednesday

G _____

L _____

A _____

D _____

S _____

Thursday

G _____

L _____

A _____

D _____

S _____

Friday

G _____

L _____

A _____

D _____

S _____

Saturday

G _____

L _____

A _____

D _____

S _____

Week Twenty-Nine
GLADS

Sunday

G _____

L _____

A _____

D _____

S _____

 **"Top GLADS" for this week:**

G _____

L _____

A _____

D _____

S _____

Aware:

Use the space below to review your week nonjudgmentally. What did you notice in your gratitude practice? Where did you do great? Where can you improve? What were the obstacles? What were the "wins"?

Assess:

Score yourself in each area below on a 1-10 scale, with 10 being "top notch!"

Physical	Emotional	Relational	Overall
_____	_____	_____	_____

Goals or ideas for improving in any of these areas:

Affirm:

Use the space below to positively acknowledge and affirm anything about yourself or your efforts from this past week:

Week Thirty

Acceptance

Everything has its wonders, even darkness and silence, and I learn, whatever state I may be in, therein to be content.

-Helen Keller

Helen Keller's life story is truly an inspiration. At 19 months of age, she contracted an illness that left her dumb, blind, and deaf, and yet she went on to become a world-famous author and speaker. Her amazing story of triumph is captured in her autobiography, The Story of My Life. Particularly beautiful is Helen Keller's description of the moment she first realized she could learn language. She writes, "I stood still, my whole attention fixed upon the motions of her fingers. Suddenly I felt a misty consciousness as of something forgotten — a thrill of returning thought; and somehow, the mystery of language was revealed to me. I knew then that w-a-t-e-r meant the wonderful cool something that was flowing over my hand. The living word awakened my soul, gave it light, hope, set it free!" I cannot imagine the joy and hope Helen Keller experienced at that very moment. Helen Keller's language ability continued to grow as she learned to sign, read lips, and ultimately speak. In her speech entitled Happiness, Helen Keller expressed gratitude for the faculties she had been given, among them, her imagination and curiosity.

Finding contentment in whatever state we are in simply means accepting what is. Accepting our gifts, our challenges, our current location, our current careers, etc. Once we accept what is, without judging it, our imagination and curiosity can be awakened to how we can use what we have been given to grow ourselves and inspire others.

What do you need to accept? Do you find yourself thinking, "If only..." or other thoughts that interfere with accepting what is? This week, see if you can non-judgementally accept wherever you are in life and open yourself to how those circumstances are growing you.

Monday

G _____

L _____

A _____

D _____

S _____

Tuesday

G _____

L _____

A _____

D _____

S _____

Wednesday

G _____

L _____

A _____

D _____

S _____

Thursday

G _____

L _____

A _____

D _____

S _____

Friday

G _____

L _____

A _____

D _____

S _____

Saturday

G _____

L _____

A _____

D _____

S _____

Week Thirty
GLADS

Sunday

G _____

L _____

A _____

D _____

S _____

"Top GLADS" for this week:

G _____

L _____

A _____

D _____

S _____

227

Aware:

Use the space below to review your week nonjudgmentally. What did you notice in your gratitude practice? Where did you do great? Where can you improve? What were the obstacles? What were the "wins"?

Assess:

Score yourself in each area below on a 1-10 scale, with 10 being "top notch!"

Physical	Emotional	Relational	Overall
_____	_____	_____	_____

Goals or ideas for improving in any of these areas:

Affirm:

Use the space below to positively acknowledge and affirm anything about yourself or your efforts from this past week:

Week Thirty-One

Adversity

Adversity introduces a man to himself.

-Albert Einstein

Nick Vujicic was born with tetra-amelia syndrome, a rare disorder characterized by the absence of arms and legs. In his autobiography, *Life Without Limits: Inspiration for a Ridiculously Good Life,* he describes both the physical and emotional battles he endured throughout childhood, adolescence, and young adulthood. At one point, he felt so alone that he even attempted to drown himself in the bathtub. He states, "For the longest, loneliest time, I wondered if there was anyone on earth like me and whether there was any purpose to my life other than pain and humiliation." A quick Google search shows that Nick is married with children, surfs, swims, travels, and inspires others. He truly lives a "ridiculously good life."

I read Nick Vujicic's story, and I still cannot fathom the adversities he has faced in his life, yet the adversities truly introduced him to himself and to millions of people around the globe. Nick is now a world-renowned motivational speaker spreading the message to find your life's purpose and never give up.

What we make of adversity determines our life path. What adversities have you faced in the past? Can you now identify how they served you? How can you be grateful for your current adversities? Try viewing adversity not as a setback but as a setup for discovering who you are. Hello you!

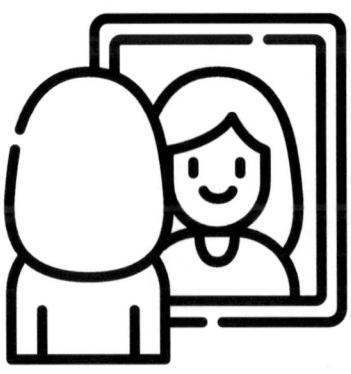

Monday

G _____

L _____

A _____

D _____

S _____

Tuesday

G _____

L _____

A _____

D _____

S _____

GLADS

Wednesday

G _____

L _____

A _____

D _____

S _____

Thursday

G _____

L _____

A _____

D _____

S _____

Friday

G _____

L _____

A _____

D _____

S _____

Saturday

G _____

L _____

A _____

D _____

S _____

Sunday

G _____

L _____

A _____

D _____

S _____

"Top GLADS" for this week:

G _____

L _____

A _____

D _____

S _____

Aware:

Use the space below to review your week nonjudgmentally. What did you notice in your gratitude practice? Where did you do great? Where can you improve? What were the obstacles? What were the "wins"?

Assess:

Score yourself in each area below on a 1-10 scale, with 10 being "top notch!"

Physical	Emotional	Relational	Overall
_____	_____	_____	_____

Goals or ideas for improving in any of these areas:

Affirm:

Use the space below to positively acknowledge and affirm anything about yourself or your efforts from this past week:

Week Thirty-Two
Acre of Diamonds

Your diamonds are not in far distant mountains or in yonder seas; they are in your own backyard if you but dig for them.

-Russell H. Conwell

Russell H. Conwell was a newspaper correspondent and later a minister during the Victorian era. He is most famous for the parable *Acres of Diamonds*. This story recounts the life of a Persian farmer who sold his farm and left his family in pursuit of wealth. He searched the world over but never found the diamonds he so desired to find. Alone, desperate, and homeless, he takes his own life. On the other hand, the man who bought the farm was grateful for what he had. He worked the land and enjoyed life with his family. One day, this man comes upon an abandoned diamond mine right there on the farm. The acre of diamonds that the previous owner had sought in despair to find had been in his backyard the entire time.

All too often, we may find ourselves looking for things that we believe are "out there." I am reminded of being stationed at an Air Force base in Oklahoma. I had desperately wanted to go anywhere but to this isolated part of the country, but it is "service before self," so my two children and I moved to Oklahoma. Once there, we had two options –make the best of it or just endure it. We settled in to learn all we could about the state of Oklahoma. We explored the Quartz Mountains and found a mom-and-pop run amusement park, we ventured to to the Wichita Mountains with their wild buffaloes and a prairie dog town. We also traveled to Red Rock Canyon and viewed it as a miniature Grand Canyon. We did day trips to Tulsa's museums and traveled along Route 66. At home, we caught crawdads from the creek that ran through the base housing area, and we rescued turtles from alongside the road and had turtle races in the backyard. We even made it an annual tradition to attend the Rattlesnake Round-Up Festival. We fully immersed ourselves in what small-town living was like in Oklahoma.

Contrast this with how some other people dealt with moving to Oklahoma. There was one young man who came into therapy for help with depression. In each session, he would go on and on about how "this [Oklahoma] is not like New York." Then there was one of my commanders who would speak negatively about Oklahoma at every turn, and as often as she could, she would escape "this awful place" and go to the neighboring state of Texas looking for something better. I am sad that they did not find the "diamonds" in Oklahoma like my children and I did. Once we accepted what we had resisted, then the diamond mine was revealed.

Sometimes it is our geographical location, sometimes, it is our relationships, and sometimes it is ourselves that we are wanting to leave in the hopes of something better. Look around. Dig deep. Can you find your acre of diamonds right where you are today?

GLADS

Monday

G _____

L _____

A _____

D _____

S _____

Tuesday

G _____

L _____

A _____

D _____

S _____

GLADS

Wednesday

G _____

L _____

A _____

D _____

S _____

Thursday

G _____

L _____

A _____

D _____

S _____

Week Thirty-Two
GLADS

Friday

G _____

L _____

A _____

D _____

S _____

Saturday

G _____

L _____

A _____

D _____

S _____

Sunday

G _____

L _____

A _____

D _____

S _____

"Top GLADS" for this week:

G _____

L _____

A _____

D _____

S _____

Aware:

Use the space below to review your week nonjudgmentally. What did you notice in your gratitude practice? Where did you do great? Where can you improve? What were the obstacles? What were the "wins"?

Assess:

Score yourself in each area below on a 1-10 scale, with 10 being "top notch!"

Physical	Emotional	Relational	Overall

Goals or ideas for improving in any of these areas:

Affirm:

Use the space below to positively acknowledge and affirm anything about yourself or your efforts from this past week:

Week Thirty-Three

Patience

Patience is not simply the ability to wait—it's how we behave while we are waiting.

-Joyce Meyer

Whenever I hear the word patience, I immediately recall a conversation with my daughter when she was five years old. I had just picked her and my son up from the aftercare program at the Air Force base where we were stationed. On this particular day, my son, who is usually very quiet, had something he wanted to share about his day but could hardly get a word in as my daughter kept interrupting him. I asked my daughter to just be patient and that I would hear her story after my son finished telling me about his day. To which she quite precociously retorted, "Mom, I can't be patient. Patience takes time!" Oh, how very true.

Patience does take time. Yet, patience is not merely waiting out the ticking of the clock or the days on the calendar. Patience is calm endurance, and in our fast-paced world, patience seems to be a dying virtue. We press the elevator button over and over, knowing it does not make the elevator come any faster. We upgrade our phone and internet plans to have an even higher speed capability. We honk our horns at drivers the second the light changes from red to green. We want things quicker, and faster, and we want them now. Won't we miss out if we are patient? Is there really any benefit to being patient?

Since life does not happen on our schedule, patience with ourselves, situations, and others is needed in order to be happy. Perhaps you are healing from a physical illness or injury. If you are impatient, you will interfere with and extend the healing process. Perhaps you are building your career. Patience will allow you to create a strong foundation that can support your dream. Perhaps you have a child who has a learning disability. Patience will allow an environment of love and acceptance that will lead to learning.

The key to patience is the story you tell yourself. Notice impatient, demanding words that you might use, such as "should, ought, have to, need to," and this week, try replacing those words with "prefer, would like, it would be nice to." This change in vocabulary can change your internal demands into the calm endurance of patience.

Monday

G _____

L _____

A _____

D _____

S _____

Tuesday

G _____

L _____

A _____

D _____

S _____

GLADS

Wednesday

G _____

L _____

A _____

D _____

S _____

Thursday

G _____

L _____

A _____

D _____

S _____

Friday

G _____

L _____

A _____

D _____

S _____

Saturday

G _____

L _____

A _____

D _____

S _____

Sunday

G _____

L _____

A _____

D _____

S _____

"Top GLADS" for this week:

G _____

L _____

A _____

D _____

S _____

Aware:

Use the space below to review your week nonjudgmentally. What did you notice in your gratitude practice? Where did you do great? Where can you improve? What were the obstacles? What were the "wins"?

Assess:

Score yourself in each area below on a 1-10 scale, with 10 being "top notch!"

Physical	Emotional	Relational	Overall

Goals or ideas for improving in any of these areas:

Affirm:

Use the space below to positively acknowledge and affirm anything about yourself or your efforts from this past week:

Week Thirty-Four
Word

Whatever words we utter should be chosen with care for people will hear them and be influenced by them for good or ill.

-Buddha

A group of frogs was traveling through the woods, and two of them fell into a deep pit. All the other frogs gathered around the pit, and seeing how deep the pit was, they told the two frogs who had fallen that they were as good as dead. The two fallen frogs ignored the comments and attempted with all of their might to jump out of the pit. As they jumped and jumped, the other frogs continued telling them to stop, that they were as good as dead.

Finally, one of the frogs took heed of what the other frogs were saying and gave up. He fell down and died. The other frog continued to jump as hard as he could. The other frogs continued to yell at him to give up, to stop the pain and just die. However, he jumped even harder and finally made it out!

You see, this frog was deaf and unable to hear the other frogs. He thought they were encouraging him the entire time. Words are powerful. They can be used to build somebody up or break somebody down.

How do you choose to use this powerful tool we call language? This week, **THINK** before you say something. Ask yourself, "Is what I am about to say: Truthful, Helpful, Inspiring, Necessary, Kind?" If not, don't kill the proverbial frog. If yes, go ahead and be part of the reason the proverbial frog succeeds!

Monday

G _____

L _____

A _____

D _____

S _____

Tuesday

G _____

L _____

A _____

D _____

S _____

Wednesday

G _____

L _____

A _____

D _____

S _____

Thursday

G _____

L _____

A _____

D _____

S _____

Friday

G _____

L _____

A _____

D _____

S _____

Saturday

G _____

L _____

A _____

D _____

S _____

Sunday

G _____

L _____

A _____

D _____

S _____

"Top GLADS" for this week:

G _____

L _____

A _____

D _____

S _____

Aware:

Use the space below to review your week nonjudgmentally. What did you notice in your gratitude practice? Where did you do great? Where can you improve? What were the obstacles? What were the "wins"?

Assess:

Score yourself in each area below on a 1-10 scale, with 10 being "top notch!"

Physical	Emotional	Relational	Overall
_____	_____	_____	_____

Goals or ideas for improving in any of these areas:

Affirm:

Use the space below to positively acknowledge and affirm anything about yourself or your efforts from this past week:

Week Thirty-Five

Hurts

Cry. Forgive. Learn. Move on. Let your tears water the seeds of your future happiness.

-Steve Maraboli

We have all been hurt, sometimes very deeply, but it is not healthy to stay stuck in the pain. Steve Maraboli, an inspirational speaker and behavior scientist, offers a very straightforward formula for how to effectively heal from our hurts. So let's explore Maraboli's formula.

First, cry. Crying is visual evidence of our pain, and each tear is a drop of pain being released from the body. To hold in your tears is to hold in your pain and therefore convert your necessary pain into unnecessary suffering. The second step is to forgive. Forgiveness is not forgetting, and it is certainly not condoning or being "okay" with whatever caused the hurt. Forgiveness is simply choosing not to remain imprisoned by anger or bitterness over what happened. It is choosing to free yourself. Whoever or whatever caused the hurt is not hurt one bit by your unforgiveness. As the saying goes, "Not forgiving is like drinking poison and expecting the other person to die." So, forgive and unlock the prison doors. The third step is to learn. What is a positive learning you can take away from this hurt? Maybe you learned that everybody is fallible or that you need to have healthier boundaries. Perhaps you learned that it is better to have hopes than expectations. Keep searching until you find the positive lesson in the hurt.

Finally, move on. To move on requires that we accept what is rather than holding on to the "why's," and "what if's". Our crying has honored our pain and released it, forgiving has freed us from the prison of anger and bitterness, learning helped us grow, and now it is time to move forward and away from the prison of hurt and unforgiveness. You are freed from the prison of pain, but you need to take the steps away from the past into the future that is waiting for you. Is there some hurt that is keeping you from your best life? If so, cry, forgive, learn, and move on.

GLADS

Monday

G _____

L _____

A _____

D _____

S _____

Tuesday

G _____

L _____

A _____

D _____

S _____

GLADS

Wednesday

G _____

L _____

A _____

D _____

S _____

Thursday

G _____

L _____

A _____

D _____

S _____

Friday

G _____

L _____

A _____

D _____

S _____

Saturday

G _____

L _____

A _____

D _____

S _____

Sunday

G _____

L _____

A _____

D _____

S _____

 "Top GLADS" for this week:

G _____

L _____

A _____

D _____

S _____

Aware:

Use the space below to review your week nonjudgmentally. What did you notice in your gratitude practice? Where did you do great? Where can you improve? What were the obstacles? What were the "wins"?

Assess:

Score yourself in each area below on a 1-10 scale, with 10 being "top notch!"

Physical	Emotional	Relational	Overall

Goals or ideas for improving in any of these areas:

Affirm:

Use the space below to positively acknowledge and affirm anything about yourself or your efforts from this past week:

Week Thirty-Six
Difficulties

In the middle of every difficulty lies opportunity.

-Albert Einstein

David Peter Cradick, known as "Kidd Kraddick" and the host of a nationally syndicated morning radio program until his untimely death in July of 2013, turned difficulty into an incredible opportunity that continues to have a life-changing impact on families today. It all started when Kidd and his wife were expecting their first child. Tests were conducted, and Kidd and his wife were told that their unborn child would be born with a chronic illness. This news, as any parent can imagine, was devastating. Fortunately, the doctors were wrong, and their daughter, Caroline, was born perfectly healthy.

Through this experience, Kidd's eyes were opened to the challenges families face when having a child with a chronic illness or other life-altering conditions. This difficulty inspired Kidd to create Kidd's Kids with the dream of making a difference in these kids' and their family's lives. In 1991, a bus filled with kids and their families headed off to Sea World, giving them a chance to do something "normal" and memorable and, for a brief moment, to forget about the challenges of their everyday lives.

Today, with combined volunteer efforts, donors, and medical professionals, along with the Kidd Kraddick Morning Show listeners' donations, Kidd's Kids has sent over 1000 kids and their families on a trip of a lifetime to Walt Disney World in Orlando, Florida...and it keeps on growing.

What difficulty are you facing? Some difficulties are small, others are big, some turn out not to be real, and some seem to stick around and never leave. With a change in perspective, your difficulty is just an opportunity in disguise. Instead of asking why, ask what you can do with it.

PERSPECTIVE

Monday

G _____

L _____

A _____

D _____

S _____

Tuesday

G _____

L _____

A _____

D _____

S _____

Wednesday

G _____

L _____

A _____

D _____

S _____

Thursday

G _____

L _____

A _____

D _____

S _____

Friday

G _____

L _____

A _____

D _____

S _____

Saturday

G _____

L _____

A _____

D _____

S _____

Sunday

G _____

L _____

A _____

D _____

S _____

"Top GLADS" for this week:

G _____

L _____

A _____

D _____

S _____

Aware:

Use the space below to review your week nonjudgmentally. What did you notice in your gratitude practice? Where did you do great? Where can you improve? What were the obstacles? What were the "wins"?

Assess:

Score yourself in each area below on a 1-10 scale, with 10 being "top notch!"

Physical	Emotional	Relational	Overall
_____	_____	_____	_____

Goals or ideas for improving in any of these areas:

Affirm:

Use the space below to positively acknowledge and affirm anything about yourself or your efforts from this past week:

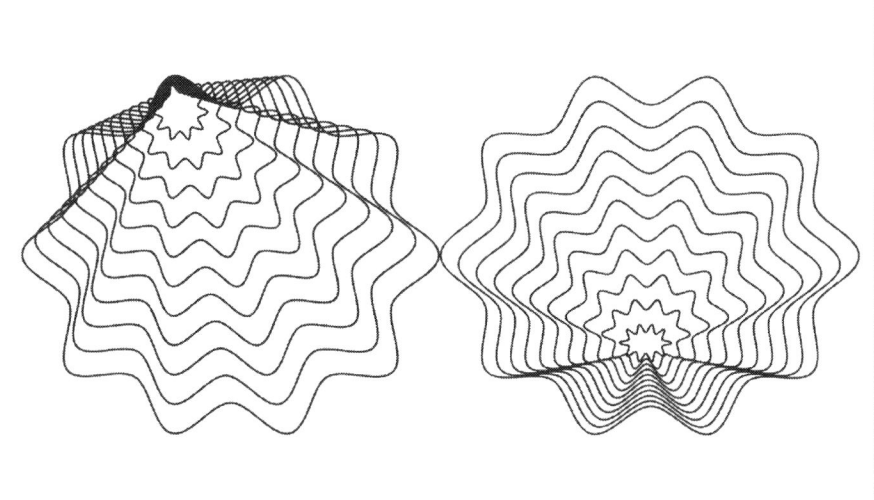

Week Thirty-Seven
Who You Are

You find peace not by rearranging the circumstances of your life, but by realizing who you are at the deepest level.

-Eckhart Tolle

One of my favorite movies is the Disney animated feature, *The Lion King*. While it is certainly beautiful in terms of animation and music, the storyline is, on one level, entertaining and, on another level, quite philosophical and existential. At the beginning of the story, Scar, the jealous brother of Mufasa, devises a plan to kill both Mufasa and Simba so that he can rule over the Pride Lands. His plan leaves Mufasa dead, but Simba survives. Scar then convinces Simba it is Simba's fault that Mufasa is dead and advises him to, "Run away and never come back." Simba, filled with guilt and turmoil, heeds his Uncle's advice and flees into exile, abandoning his identity as the future king.

Simba's childhood passes by as he wanders around with a meerkat and warthog, changing his circumstances with the motto of "Hakuna Matata," which means no worries, as he tries to forget who he is and what has happened. And then it happens. Through a series of events, Simba is led to a body of water in which he sees his reflection, and for a moment he believes he is seeing his father. When he looks again, he realizes it is not his father, Mufasa, in the water, but his own reflection. Then he hears the unmistakable, booming, regal voice of his father from the heavens stating, "You have forgotten who you are, and so have forgotten me. Look inside yourself, Simba. You are more than what you have become."

By the end of the film (spoiler alert), Simba does, in fact, remember who he is. He is the son of Mufasa. He was born to be king. He leaves the "Hakuna Matata" life, makes peace with his past, and overcomes challenges, and Simba takes his rightful place as The Lion King.

This week, stop the hustle and bustle and attempts to control and arrange your circumstances. Take some time to look inside yourself. Remember who you are, take your rightful place in your life, and there within, find the peace you seek to find.

Monday

G _____

L _____

A _____

D _____

S _____

Tuesday

G _____

L _____

A _____

D _____

S _____

Wednesday

G _____

L _____

A _____

D _____

S _____

Thursday

G _____

L _____

A _____

D _____

S _____

Friday

G _____

L _____

A _____

D _____

S _____

Saturday

G _____

L _____

A _____

D _____

S _____

Sunday

G _____

L _____

A _____

D _____

S _____

 "Top GLADS" for this week:

G _____

L _____

A _____

D _____

S _____

Aware:

Use the space below to review your week nonjudgmentally. What did you notice in your gratitude practice? Where did you do great? Where can you improve? What were the obstacles? What were the "wins"?

Assess:

Score yourself in each area below on a 1-10 scale, with 10 being "top notch!"

Physical	Emotional	Relational	Overall

Goals or ideas for improving in any of these areas:

Affirm:

Use the space below to positively acknowledge and affirm anything about yourself or your efforts from this past week:

Week Thirty-Eight

Hope

We must accept finite disappointment, but never lose infinite hope.

-Martin Luther King

Once there was a man who had become so disappointed with his career and relationships that he simply walked away from everything. He ventured out into the woods to seek advice from a wise elder. He explained his disappointments to the elder and then asked, "Do you see any reason for me not to quit? I see no hope."

The wise elder asked the man, "Do you see the bamboo and the fern here in the woods?" The man replied, "Yes." The wise elder stated that he had planted the fern seeds and the bamboo seeds at the same time and had taken good care of each of them. The wise elder stated the fern had quickly begun to grow and spread across the floor of the woods, but nothing came from the bamboo seed. Still, he continued to take good care of the bamboo seed. By the second year, the fern had flourished, and still, nothing had come from the bamboo seed. Yet, the wise elder had continued to care for the bamboo seed. Years three and four went by with the fern continuing to become more vibrant, and still, nothing from the bamboo seed, but the wise elder still did not give up on it.

Finally, in the fifth year, a small shoot sprout up from the bamboo seed. It did not look like much compared to the fern, but there was something, and the wise elder had continued to care for it. But in the sixth year, the bamboo grew to sixty feet tall. "You see," explained the wise elder, "the bamboo had spent five years growing roots to sustain the future growth."

Maybe you are at a place right now where you are disappointed that certain things have not happened or turned out as you had hoped. Perhaps you feel weary from trying and struggling and not seeing a positive result. I can tell you that even if you are not seeing what you hoped for, your efforts are not in vain. Those efforts are giving you what you will need in the future. Keep nurturing your seeds, don't give up, and when the time is right, you will sprout!

Monday

G _____

L _____

A _____

D _____

S _____

Tuesday

G _____

L _____

A _____

D _____

S _____

GLADS

Wednesday

G _____

L _____

A _____

D _____

S _____

Thursday

G _____

L _____

A _____

D _____

S _____

Friday

G _____

L _____

A _____

D _____

S _____

Saturday

G _____

L _____

A _____

D _____

S _____

Sunday

G _____

L _____

A _____

D _____

S _____

"Top GLADS" for this week:

G _____

L _____

A _____

D _____

S _____

Aware:

Use the space below to review your week nonjudgmentally. What did you notice in your gratitude practice? Where did you do great? Where can you improve? What were the obstacles? What were the "wins"?

Assess:

Score yourself in each area below on a 1-10 scale, with 10 being "top notch!"

Physical	Emotional	Relational	Overall
_____	_____	_____	_____

Goals or ideas for improving in any of these areas:

Affirm:

Use the space below to positively acknowledge and affirm anything about yourself or your efforts from this past week:

Week Thirty-Nine
Power of Thought

Today is the father of tomorrow.

-Charles F. Stanley

Looking at your life, have you ever thought, "How did I get here?" This question can be asked from a place of wonder or a place of pain, but either way, the answer is the same. Where you are today is the result of your past ways of thinking and behaving. Do you like where you are? If yes, continue doing what you have been doing. If your answer is no or maybe a mix of yes and no, then first take a look at your thoughts. Any of our thoughts, if thought of often enough, become our actions, and our actions become our habits, and our habits become our character.

Remember the children's storybook, *The Little Engine* That Could? In the story, there is a large train filled with toys and gifts for little boys and girls, but the train breaks down before it can deliver the toys to the children. After the broken-down train asks several passing trains for help over the mountain, and none are willing to help, a little blue engine agrees to help get the stranded toys to the children. Even though she is small, the little blue engine tries her best to bring the toys to the children on the other side of the hill. She has a mission. She knows where she wants and needs to go. The load feels heavier as she chugs up the hill, and the mission gets very difficult. Rather than quitting, she reminds herself of her mission and repeatedly says, "I think I can. I think I can. I think I can." This thought fuels her actions, and she slowly chugs bit by bit up the steep mountain. As she nears the top, filled with eager excitement, she exclaims, "I know I can. I know I can. I know I can!" And she triumphantly reaches her goal. The little engine thought she could, believed she could, and then she did.

Do you know what you want to achieve? Do you know the type of person you want to be? Are your thoughts and actions moving you closer to that goal? This week, notice what your mental chatter is saying to you. Be mindful of how those thoughts are influencing your actions or inactions. How are they shaping your character? Are they creating the tomorrow you hope to find?

Monday

G _____

L _____

A _____

D _____

S _____

Tuesday

G _____

L _____

A _____

D _____

S _____

Wednesday

G _____

L _____

A _____

D _____

S _____

Thursday

G _____

L _____

A _____

D _____

S _____

Friday

G _____

L _____

A _____

D _____

S _____

Saturday

G _____

L _____

A _____

D _____

S _____

Sunday

G _____

L _____

A _____

D _____

S _____

"Top GLADS" for this week:

G _____

L _____

A _____

D _____

S _____

Aware:

Use the space below to review your week nonjudgmentally. What did you notice in your gratitude practice? Where did you do great? Where can you improve? What were the obstacles? What were the "wins"?

Assess:

Score yourself in each area below on a 1-10 scale, with 10 being "top notch!"

Physical	Emotional	Relational	Overall
_____	_____	_____	_____

Goals or ideas for improving in any of these areas:

Affirm:

Use the space below to positively acknowledge and affirm anything about yourself or your efforts from this past week:

Week Forty
Why? to What?

Nothing ever goes away until it teaches us what we need to know.

-Pema Chodron

When a problem occurs, we generally want to understand why it happened so we can prevent it from happening again. One strategy is to conduct a root cause analysis. You have likely conducted a root cause analysis, even if you didn't know that is what it is called. A root cause analysis is a method of problem-solving used for identifying the root causes of faults or problems to understand why the problem occurred in the first place and then using the data to devise a plan to prevent the problem from happening again. It is widely used in IT operations, telecommunications, industrial process control, accident analysis, and the healthcare industry. One root cause analysis strategy (and the one you have probably done informally is "the five why's," which consists of asking the question, "Why did this problem happen?" and then repeatedly asking, "But why?" until you get to the root cause of the problem.

While a root cause analysis can be helpful in our personal lives when we are trying to find the reason for a specific problem, such as repeated tardiness to work, it is often not an effective technique for understanding life situations. Life situations are not meant to be solved; they are not solvable. Life situations are complicated, (e.g., the death of a loved one, or a chronic illness) and do not have one specific root cause. If we try to find the cause, we will get sucked into the never-ending spiral of "why's" with no satisfactory answer. Specific problems are meant to be solved to avoid repeating the same mistakes. Life situations are not meant to be solved; they are intended to be accepted so we can grow in and from them.

We would make better use of our time and energy if we changed our questioning regarding life situations from "Why is this happening? Why me? Why now?" to "What can I learn from this?" or, as Oprah Winfrey has stated, "Why is this happening *for* me?" Because, let's face it, if we ever really could understand the "why" of our circumstances, we will still have to figure out the "what."

This week, check in with your "why's" and see if you would do better changing the "why's" to "what…"

Monday

G _____

L _____

A _____

D _____

S _____

Tuesday

G _____

L _____

A _____

D _____

S _____

Week Fourty
GLADS

Wednesday

G _____

L _____

A _____

D _____

S _____

Thursday

G _____

L _____

A _____

D _____

S _____

Friday

G _____

L _____

A _____

D _____

S _____

Saturday

G _____

L _____

A _____

D _____

S _____

Week Fourty
GLADS

Sunday

G _____

L _____

A _____

D _____

S _____

 "Top GLADS" for this week:

G _____

L _____

A _____

D _____

S _____

Aware:

Use the space below to review your week nonjudgmentally. What did you notice in your gratitude practice? Where did you do great? Where can you improve? What were the obstacles? What were the "wins"?

Assess:

Score yourself in each area below on a 1-10 scale, with 10 being "top notch!"

Physical	Emotional	Relational	Overall
_____	_____	_____	_____

Goals or ideas for improving in any of these areas:

Affirm:

Use the space below to positively acknowledge and affirm anything about yourself or your efforts from this past week:

Week Forty-One
Relationships

We are born in relationship. We grow in relationship. We are wounded in relationship. And we are healed in relationship.

-Harville Hendrix

Relationships of all kinds can be challenging. Sometimes we may even question whether being in a relationship with others is worth it. Yet we all continue seeking new relationships and engaging in our current ones. It is as if, intuitively, we know that we are better off when we are connected to others. Science backs this up. Research shows that relational well-being leads to increased social support, decreased stress, better overall health, and increased longevity.

So, what exactly is relational wellness, and how do we improve it? Relational wellness requires connecting and interacting with others in such a way that we create nurturing and supportive relationships. This is not something that happens haphazardly. This is something that requires intention, awareness, and action.

I am reminded of my first effort to grow flowers. I was in my early twenties and thought a wildflower garden would look lovely out in my yard. I had visions of bright blooms, sweet smells, bumble bees, and ladybugs. I could just see myself stepping outside my front door, garden shears in hand, cutting a bouquet of flowers to place in a vase of water on top of my dining room table. I purchased several packets of wildflower seeds and scattered them onto a pile of dirt and sprinkled them with water. I waited. I watered the seeds and waited some more. Weeks went by with not a seedling in sight. Eventually, a few popped up here and there, but by the end of the summer, my dreams of a wildflower garden were as dead as the few flowers that managed to grow from this haphazard attempt at an English wildflower garden.

What had gone wrong with my wildflower garden? The same thing went wrong that can go wrong in our relationships. You see, I had the *intention* of growing a flower garden; however, I approached it with only partial *awareness*. I knew I wanted flowers, but I did not take the time to discover what flowers were right for where I lived. I did not pay attention to what was necessary for flowers to grow—the timing, climate, soil, sun, etc. Having the intention to create new relationships or grow our current relationships is not enough. We first need to know ourselves and be aware of our relationship needs. What kind of people do we want in our lives? How many friends work best for us? How am I as a friend? Once we know what types of relationships we want in our lives, we must put in the work. This requires attention to the needs of each relationship and proper action to meet those needs.

Like flowers, where too much or too little water can be harmful, so it is with relationships regarding how much or how little time, effort, and give-and-take we give each relationship. And, just like a flower garden, a growing, healthy relationship requires you to keep the intention of having a relationship, maintain awareness of what is happening in the relationship, and give proper attention to the changing needs of the relationship. Are you giving the right amount of time to your relationships? Where are you in your relational wellness? What needs your attention?

Week Forty-One
GLADS

Monday

G _____

L _____

A _____

D _____

S _____

Tuesday

G _____

L _____

A _____

D _____

S _____

Wednesday

G _____

L _____

A _____

D _____

S _____

Thursday

G _____

L _____

A _____

D _____

S _____

Friday

G _____

L _____

A _____

D _____

S _____

Saturday

G _____

L _____

A _____

D _____

S _____

Sunday

G _____

L _____

A _____

D _____

S _____

"Top GLADS" for this week:

G _____

L _____

A _____

D _____

S _____

Aware:

Use the space below to review your week nonjudgmentally. What did you notice in your gratitude practice? Where did you do great? Where can you improve? What were the obstacles? What were the "wins"?

Assess:

Score yourself in each area below on a 1-10 scale, with 10 being "top notch!"

Physical	Emotional	Relational	Overall
_____	_____	_____	_____

Goals or ideas for improving in any of these areas:

Affirm:

Use the space below to positively acknowledge and affirm anything about yourself or your efforts from this past week:

Week Forty-Two

Creativity

To live a creative life, we must lose our fear of being wrong.

-Joshua Chilton Pearce

What is creativity? Creativity is the ability to perceive the world in new ways, make connections between seemingly unrelated phenomena, and generate solutions. Simply put, it is the act of turning new and imagined ideas into reality. Children are great at this. Have you seen all of the things a child can do with a simple box? What did you last do with a box? Somewhere, we have lost our creativity. In fact, this is evidenced by a longitudinal study on creativity conducted by George Land. This study revealed that between the ages of five years, ten years, and 15 years of age, scores on a creativity test dropped from 98% to 30% to only 12%, respectively. Another study on creativity in adults showed that adults only scored 2% on a creativity test. Clearly, we have all but lost our creativity.

Is creativity important? Absolutely! When we are creative, we are better problem solvers, we are more adaptable, and we have an increased sense of our uniqueness. Additionally, research shows that creativity decreases vulnerability to negative emotions such as depression and anxiety. In summary, creativity is a vital part of our holistic wellness that, unfortunately, is not nurtured throughout adulthood.

Can you re-learn creativity? Yes! Remember, creativity is the ability to perceive the world in new ways. There are many exercises you can do to help you do this. For example, pick an object and list everything you could do with that object. When you think you have an exhaustive list, take a break for an hour. After an hour, see how many other things you can come up with for that same object. Another idea, make a squiggle on a piece of paper and pass it around between two to three people, with each person adding to the squiggle to create something. Other things you can do to increase your ability to be creative indirectly include taking a different route home, using a color you don't typically like, trying a new food item, mixing and matching your clothes differently, etc. The idea is to do things differently, to see things differently. What can you do this week to increase your creativity?

Monday

G _____

L _____

A _____

D _____

S _____

Tuesday

G _____

L _____

A _____

D _____

S _____

Wednesday

G _____

L _____

A _____

D _____

S _____

Thursday

G _____

L _____

A _____

D _____

S _____

Friday

G _____

L _____

A _____

D _____

S _____

Saturday

G _____

L _____

A _____

D _____

S _____

Sunday

G _____

L _____

A _____

D _____

S _____

"Top GLADS" for this week:

G _____

L _____

A _____

D _____

S _____

Aware:

Use the space below to review your week nonjudgmentally. What did you notice in your gratitude practice? Where did you do great? Where can you improve? What were the obstacles? What were the "wins"?

Assess:

Score yourself in each area below on a 1-10 scale, with 10 being "top notch!"

Physical	Emotional	Relational	Overall
_____	_____	_____	_____

Goals or ideas for improving in any of these areas:

Affirm:

Use the space below to positively acknowledge and affirm anything about yourself or your efforts from this past week:

Week Forty-Three
Where's Your Focus?

Consult not your fears but your hopes and your dreams. Think not about your frustrations, but about your unfulfilled potential. Concern yourself not with what you tried and failed in, but with what it is still possible for you to do.

-Pope John Paul XXII

Regardless of how much we try to control life, we ultimately do not have control over our circumstances. We do, however, have control over how we choose to view those circumstances and what we choose to focus on.

There is a story of a college professor who surprised his students with an unscheduled exam. On the students' desks was a sheet of paper, and when the professor gave the word, they turned over the paper. On the paper was one black dot. The professor instructed the students to write about what they saw. After fifteen minutes, the professor collected the written responses from the students and read each of them out loud. Every one of the students had written about the black dot—the size, the position, etc. After reading the students' responses, he noted out loud that none of them had written about the white space on the paper. He told the students he had never intended to grade the exams; instead, he wanted to give them something to think about.

Life certainly has its share of black dots. What would happen if today you took your eyes away from the black dots in your life and instead focused on the white paper? What if you focused not on your fears but on your hopes? Not on your frustrations but on your potential? Not on your failures but on the lessons learned? We all have a white piece of paper to observe and enjoy. Only you can choose whether to focus on the dark dots or on the white space.

Monday

G _____

L _____

A _____

D _____

S _____

Tuesday

G _____

L _____

A _____

D _____

S _____

Wednesday

G _____

L _____

A _____

D _____

S _____

Thursday

G _____

L _____

A _____

D _____

S _____

Friday

G _____

L _____

A _____

D _____

S _____

Saturday

G _____

L _____

A _____

D _____

S _____

Sunday

G _____

L _____

A _____

D _____

S _____

"Top GLADS" for this week:

G _____

L _____

A _____

D _____

S _____

Aware:

Use the space below to review your week nonjudgmentally. What did you notice in your gratitude practice? Where did you do great? Where can you improve? What were the obstacles? What were the "wins"?

Assess:

Score yourself in each area below on a 1-10 scale, with 10 being "top notch!"

Physical	Emotional	Relational	Overall
_____	_____	_____	_____

Goals or ideas for improving in any of these areas:

Affirm:

Use the space below to positively acknowledge and affirm anything about yourself or your efforts from this past week:

POSITIVE

NEGATIVE

Week Forty-Four

Rejection

Rejection is nothing more than a necessary step in the pursuit of success.

-Bo Bennett

At my house, when we do laundry, we typically end up with a couple of "extra" socks (a more positive way of saying we end up with socks missing). These socks have no mate and are thrown into a laundry basket with other single socks. After several weeks, this basket containing unpaired socks gets to be full, and I will sit down on the sofa, dump out all of the socks, and begin the sorting/matching process. I will create a pile of men's dress socks, men's athletic socks, women's dress socks, women's athletic socks, boy's dress socks, boy's athletic socks, girl's dress socks, and girl's athletic socks. Then I begin sorting through each pile to find the right match-up of socks. It is a bit like the childhood game of "Match," where you turn over cards to see if you have a match.

So it was on a particular Saturday, as I sat sorting through the socks, that I realized something. I was working on my pile of socks—dress socks and athletic socks. Before me was a fantastic, name-brand dress sock I had owned for easily over a year. As I saw this sock, I thought, "What an excellent sock this is. It has gone through multiple wearings and washings and even been through a dryer cycle or two, and the nylon has retained its stretchiness. This sock stays up on my leg, and there is no sign of pilling or snagging. What a great sock this is!"

On top of the neighboring sock pile was my ergonomically designed, shock-absorbing, light-weight running sock that, at the time of purchase, I thought was overpriced for a sock—regardless of how much science went into making it! But, just as with the dress sock, I realized, "This sock is amazing. It has protected my feet through miles and miles of runs. It has taken the pounding of training runs for a marathon and been washed repeatedly; still, the sock is in great shape. What quality!"

And so, side by side, I have these two wonderful, high-quality socks, neither one better nor worse than the other, yet I did not pair them up. No. No matter how wonderful each sock is, they simply are not a match and I have never worn the two together.

In life, we have all been "rejected," whether in sports, academics, careers, or relationships. When was the last time you felt rejected? Did you take it as a hit to your self-worth? Or were you aware that rejection simply means "not a match"? When we correctly reframe "rejection" to "not the right match," we can move forward, self-worth intact, knowing we are one step closer to finding the perfect match for us.

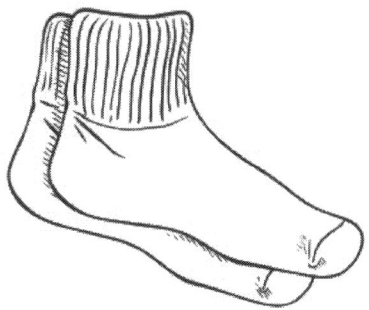

Monday

G _____

L _____

A _____

D _____

S _____

Tuesday

G _____

L _____

A _____

D _____

S _____

Wednesday

G _____

L _____

A _____

D _____

S _____

Thursday

G _____

L _____

A _____

D _____

S _____

GLADS

Friday

G _____

L _____

A _____

D _____

S _____

Saturday

G _____

L _____

A _____

D _____

S _____

Week Forty-Four
GLADS

Sunday

G _____

L _____

A _____

D _____

S _____

 "Top GLADS" for this week:

G _____

L _____

A _____

D _____

S _____

Aware:

Use the space below to review your week nonjudgmentally. What did you notice in your gratitude practice? Where did you do great? Where can you improve? What were the obstacles? What were the "wins"?

Assess:

Score yourself in each area below on a 1-10 scale, with 10 being "top notch!"

Physical	Emotional	Relational	Overall
_____	_____	_____	_____

Goals or ideas for improving in any of these areas:

Affirm:

Use the space below to positively acknowledge and affirm anything about yourself or your efforts from this past week:

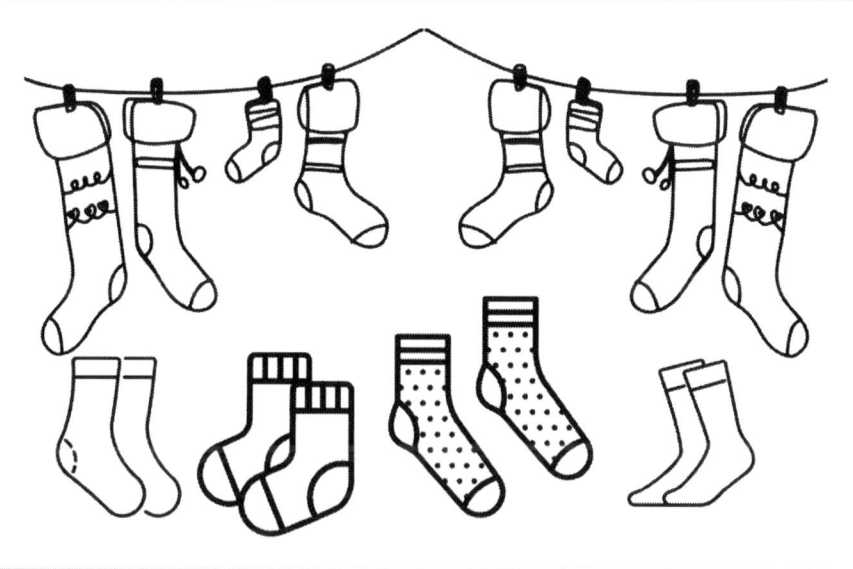

Week Forty-Five

Community

The greatness of a community is most accurately measured by the compassionate actions of its members.

-Coretta Scott King

Today I was reminded of this quote as I took my morning walk with my two Hungarian Puli dogs, Rebel and Rowser. As I write this, we are in the throes of the COVID-19 pandemic and under quarantine guidelines meaning our schools, gyms, restaurants, and other "non-essential" businesses remain closed. Typically, there would be a buzz in the air regarding upcoming proms and school graduation ceremonies —all of which have been canceled for the health and safety of everyone. We have been ordered to wear face masks in public places and keep 6 feet of distance between ourselves and others. While many adhere to these instructions for their own protection or the protection of the more vulnerable, there are still some who balk at the instructions, citing their personal rights.

There is a delicate balance between upholding our personal rights and taking care of our community. Strong arguments could be made for both sides. Having served in our U.S. Armed Forces to protect our freedoms, I understand the value of those individual rights. I also know that for our Armed Forces to protect individual rights, military members give up certain personal rights of their own for the good of our country.

As I pondered both sides of the argument, I realized the value of bringing compassion into weighing the "rightness" of either side. Individuals do not disagree merely to disagree. Each person has a personal history that leads them to view things one way or another. Unfortunately, the differences in personal history seemed to create such a divide that it truly saddened me. I wondered what this said about our community's strength and our country's future.

And then I saw homemade posters in people's yards--congratulations posters for graduating seniors and appreciation posters thanking teachers and medical personnel for their service and dedication. I saw teddy bears that people have placed in their yards so children can go for "bear hunt" walks. I saw sidewalk chalk art of rainbows and promises of better days. These things are how we measure our greatness. We accept differences with attitudes of compassion. We grow in greatness with acts of compassion, no matter how big or small they may seem. Each one adds to our communities' strength and our nation's greatness.

This week, consider how you are currently contributing to the greatness of your community. Is there something more that you can do? If so, why wait? Begin it now, and trust that you are making a difference!

Monday

G _____

L _____

A _____

D _____

S _____

Tuesday

G _____

L _____

A _____

D _____

S _____

Wednesday

G _____

L _____

A _____

D _____

S _____

Thursday

G _____

L _____

A _____

D _____

S _____

Friday

G _____

L _____

A _____

D _____

S _____

Saturday

G _____

L _____

A _____

D _____

S _____

Sunday

G _____

L _____

A _____

D _____

S _____

"Top GLADS" for this week:

G _____

L _____

A _____

D _____

S _____

Aware:

Use the space below to review your week nonjudgmentally. What did you notice in your gratitude practice? Where did you do great? Where can you improve? What were the obstacles? What were the "wins"?

Assess:

Score yourself in each area below on a 1-10 scale, with 10 being "top notch!"

Physical	Emotional	Relational	Overall

Goals or ideas for improving in any of these areas:

Affirm:

Use the space below to positively acknowledge and affirm anything about yourself or your efforts from this past week:

Week Forty-Six

Expectations

Maybe it wasn't the lack of achievements that made her and her brother's parents unhappy; maybe it was the expectation to achieve in the first place.

-Matt Haig

Expectations. An expectation is a strong belief that something will happen. For example, if a traffic light turns red, you expect that cars will stop. If it is your anniversary, you expect your spouse to have something special planned or purchased to celebrate. Expectations are helpful if what we expect to happen actually happens. Cars stop, ok. The anniversary is celebrated, ok. But what if what we expect does not happen? Uh-oh. Unmet expectations can create all kinds of difficulties—car accidents, relationship arguments, etc. Herein lies the problem with expectations—if what we expect happens, life goes on unchanged—no cause for alarm, no reason for celebration, no big deal. If what we expect does not occur, we experience disappointment, harm, or other negative consequences. So, is there an alternative?

In *The Midnight Library*, the main character gets to try out many different lives for herself. In these lives, she and her family members experience varied degrees of success and achievements, and despite the achievements, no one seems any happier in one life than in another. This leads to the insightful quote regarding expectations that the *expectation* of achievement was at the root of unhappiness. When we expect something, and it happens, there is no celebration because what happened was precisely what was supposed to happen. No one celebrates when we, or others, simply do what is expected.

Since happiness is not derived from having our expectations met, is there an alternative to having expectations? Absolutely! The alternative is to replace "expectation" with "hope." Reflect on a time when you had hoped something would happen—and then it did. What do you recall feeling? I am willing to bet you felt happy, excited, joyful, or some other positive emotion. Now, take that same situation and reflect on how you would have felt if what happened had been an "expectation" rather than a "hope." See the difference?

My challenge for you is to look over your expectations list, change them to hopes, and take note of what happens. Need help to determine what your expectations are? Notice when you are disappointed or upset about something, then ask yourself, "What did I think was going to happen?" Now you have uncovered a hidden expectation, and you can now turn that expectation into a hope.

Monday

G _____

L _____

A _____

D _____

S _____

Tuesday

G _____

L _____

A _____

D _____

S _____

Wednesday

G _____

L _____

A _____

D _____

S _____

Thursday

G _____

L _____

A _____

D _____

S _____

Friday

G _____

L _____

A _____

D _____

S _____

Saturday

G _____

L _____

A _____

D _____

S _____

Sunday

G _____

L _____

A _____

D _____

S _____

 **"Top GLADS" for this week:**

G _____

L _____

A _____

D _____

S _____

Aware:

Use the space below to review your week nonjudgmentally. What did you notice in your gratitude practice? Where did you do great? Where can you improve? What were the obstacles? What were the "wins"?

Assess:

Score yourself in each area below on a 1-10 scale, with 10 being "top notch!"

Physical	Emotional	Relational	Overall
_____	_____	_____	_____

Goals or ideas for improving in any of these areas:

Affirm:

Use the space below to positively acknowledge and affirm anything about yourself or your efforts from this past week:

Week Forty-Seven

Learning

Learning should commence at birth and cease only with death.

-Albert Einstein

What comes to mind when you think of learning? For many, it is images of sitting in a classroom or library, straining away at a lesson, wishing you were anywhere but there do anything besides studying. And Einstein says this should only cease with death? Some of you may be groaning at the thought. Well, here is some good news. Learning does not always have to involve school, books, lectures, etc. And Einstein agreed. After winning the Nobel Prize for his theory of general relativity, Einstein wrote this excerpt in a letter to his 11-year-old son, Hans Albert:

"...I am very pleased that you find joy with the piano. This and carpentry are, in my opinion, for your age the best pursuits, better even than school. Because those are things which fit a young person such as you very well. Mainly play the things on the piano which please you, even if the teacher does not assign those. That is the way to learn the most, that when you are doing something with such enjoyment that you don't notice that the time passes. I am sometimes so wrapped up in my work that I forget about the noon meal. Also, play ringtoss with Tete. That teaches you agility..."

The greatest of thinkers understood the priceless role of play in our learning and growing experience. This week, take the advice from a genius and engage in learning in the way you can learn the most by "doing something with such enjoyment that you don't notice that the time passes."

Monday

G _____

L _____

A _____

D _____

S _____

Tuesday

G _____

L _____

A _____

D _____

S _____

Wednesday

G _____

L _____

A _____

D _____

S _____

Thursday

G _____

L _____

A _____

D _____

S _____

Friday

G _____

L _____

A _____

D _____

S _____

Saturday

G _____

L _____

A _____

D _____

S _____

Sunday

G _____

L _____

A _____

D _____

S _____

"Top GLADS" for this week:

G _____

L _____

A _____

D _____

S _____

Aware:

Use the space below to review your week nonjudgmentally. What did you notice in your gratitude practice? Where did you do great? Where can you improve? What were the obstacles? What were the "wins"?

Assess:

Score yourself in each area below on a 1-10 scale, with 10 being "top notch!"

Physical	Emotional	Relational	Overall
_____	_____	_____	_____

Goals or ideas for improving in any of these areas:

Affirm:

Use the space below to positively acknowledge and affirm anything about yourself or your efforts from this past week:

Week Forty-Eight
Celebrating Moments

Be happy for this moment. This moment is your life.

-Omar Khayyam

How easy it is to get caught up in the hustle and bustle of daily life. We have our schedules and "to-do" lists, and there is always something "out there" to look forward to. Many of us believe, "I will be happy when...," fill in the blank with, "when I lose those last five pounds," or "when I get that promotion," or "when we can finally retire."

Sadly, this approach to life robs us of our lives because we are always waiting for, striving for, or wanting more rather than basking in the joy of the present moment. I recognize that my "striving for" approach has robbed me of celebrating moments that were most definitely worthy of celebration. I did not allow myself to fully celebrate the accomplishments of earning a bachelor's degree, a master's degree, or even a doctorate because there was always yet another step to take. I cannot regain these moments, but I have learned a valuable lesson from missing them. I have learned that while it is essential to have goals and continue to strive towards achieving them, it is equally as important to pause and look back at where you've come from and celebrate where you are at this very moment.

A Chinese Proverb states, "The best time to plant a tree was twenty years ago. The second best time is now." Perhaps, like me, you have missed being happy in some of the key moments that have made up your life. None of us can go back, but we can be here, now, in the present. Throughout this week, in whatever you do, stop. Notice what is around you at that very moment. In fact, right now, stop. Notice who you are in this moment and all that has led up to this moment. Breathe into it, for there will never be another moment like this one. Celebrate it! Celebrate you!

Monday

G _____

L _____

A _____

D _____

S _____

Tuesday

G _____

L _____

A _____

D _____

S _____

Wednesday

G _____

L _____

A _____

D _____

S _____

Thursday

G _____

L _____

A _____

D _____

S _____

Friday

G _____

L _____

A _____

D _____

S _____

Saturday

G _____

L _____

A _____

D _____

S _____

Week Forty-Eight
GLADS

Sunday

G _____

L _____

A _____

D _____

S _____

"Top GLADS" for this week:

G _____

L _____

A _____

D _____

S _____

Aware:

Use the space below to review your week nonjudgmentally. What did you notice in your gratitude practice? Where did you do great? Where can you improve? What were the obstacles? What were the "wins"?

Assess:

Score yourself in each area below on a 1-10 scale, with 10 being "top notch!"

Physical	Emotional	Relational	Overall
_____	_____	_____	_____

Goals or ideas for improving in any of these areas:

Affirm:

Use the space below to positively acknowledge and affirm anything about yourself or your efforts from this past week:

Week Forty-Nine
Giving and Receiving

When we give cheerfully and accept gratefully, everyone is blessed.

-Maya Angelou

Are you a cheerful giver? I am reminded of Russell and Lillian Hoban's endearing story, *A Birthday for Frances.* In the story, Frances' little sister is having a birthday, and Frances uses her money to purchase a *Chompo* bar for Gloria's birthday gift. Throughout the story, Frances is disgruntled about having to give her sister the *Chompo* bar and feels resentful towards her sister. At the birthday party, Frances sings: "Happy *Chompo* to me, is how it ought to be," --not exactly a cheerful giver! By the end of the story, Frances has had a reluctant change of heart from watching other children happily give their gifts to Gloria, and Frances is finally able to give her sister the *Chompo* bar and wish her a happy birthday.

Disgruntled giving results in resentment, and resentment is poison to relationships. When we give, whether it is giving material things or our time, we need to do so with a joyful heart; otherwise, it would be better for the other person and us if we did not give at all.

Perhaps you are an excellent giver. How are you as a receiver? Many phrases are used out of politeness when we receive something that actually diminishes the giving experience for both the giver and us. For example, someone takes time to find just the perfect gift for you, and they are excited to see your expression of joy when you receive the gift. Then, perhaps you reply by saying, "Oh, you shouldn't have!" or "This is way too expensive. You didn't *need* to get me this." But they didn't need to get you that gift, they *wanted* to get it for you. Or, someone compliments your dress, and you reply, "Oh, I've had this for a while." These replies interfere with our ability to soak in the joy that accompanies receiving a gift or a compliment or an offer of help, and we have robbed the other person of the full joy encompassed in the gift-giving experience.

This week, open yourself up to the full giving-receiving cycle. As you give cheerfully and accept gratefully, you and all of your relationships will be truly blessed!

Monday

G _____

L _____

A _____

D _____

S _____

Tuesday

G _____

L _____

A _____

D _____

S _____

Wednesday

G _____

L _____

A _____

D _____

S _____

Thursday

G _____

L _____

A _____

D _____

S _____

Friday

G _____

L _____

A _____

D _____

S _____

Saturday

G _____

L _____

A _____

D _____

S _____

Sunday

G _____

L _____

A _____

D _____

S _____

"Top GLADS" for this week:

G _____

L _____

A _____

D _____

S _____

Aware:

Use the space below to review your week nonjudgmentally. What did you notice in your gratitude practice? Where did you do great? Where can you improve? What were the obstacles? What were the "wins"?

Assess:

Score yourself in each area below on a 1-10 scale, with 10 being "top notch!"

Physical	Emotional	Relational	Overall
_____	_____	_____	_____

Goals or ideas for improving in any of these areas:

Affirm:

Use the space below to positively acknowledge and affirm anything about yourself or your efforts from this past week:

Week Fifty
Date Palms

Maybe God created the desert so man could appreciate the date palms.

--Paulo Coelho

You undoubtedly know what a desert is. A desert is a vast, dry area of land with little precipitation. The landscape is rather barren, and conditions can be pretty hostile. Deserts can feel lonely, hopeless, and never-ending. But do you know much about date palms? It turns out that date palms are pretty interesting. Fossil records indicate date palms have existed for at least 50 million years in the harsh desert conditions of what we now refer to as the Middle East. Every bit of a date palm is usable; nothing is wasted. The fruit can be enjoyed soft or dried, and the seeds can be ground and used similarly to coffee. Green date leaves can be cooked and eaten like a vegetable, and mature leaves can be used to make mats, fans, and baskets. The leaf sheaths can be used for rope, coarse cloth, and large hats. A date palm is a very useful tree, but the date palm also has significant symbolic meaning. Throughout history, date palms have symbolized honesty and righteousness in major world religions, such as Christianity, Judaism, and Islam. The ancient Egyptians revered the tree as representing fertility, whereas Ancient Romans used date palms to symbolize prosperity and triumph.

It is in the desert on his way to achieving his "personal legend" that Santiago, the protagonist in *The Alchemist,* comes upon a date palm tree and has the thought, "Maybe God created the desert so man could appreciate the date palms." Like Santiago, we have all, at some point, found ourselves in our own personal desert. Perhaps you are in a desert now. Maybe on your journey, you knew you would need to go through a desert (or two), or maybe you were completely surprised to find yourself in a desert. Whatever the case, a desert is not likely where you want to be, yet it is precisely where you need to be. Santiago came upon the date palm in the desert. The desert is where Santiago learned to be mindful of every bit of creation around him and realized that he is a part of nature and a part of God and, therefore, able to accomplish miracles.

Be in your desert. Whatever you need to discover is right there in that seemingly lonely and hopeless place. Somewhere in your desert is a date palm promising prosperity and triumph. Remember to enjoy a date or two while you are there.

Week Fifty
GLADS

Monday

G _____

L _____

A _____

D _____

S _____

Tuesday

G _____

L _____

A _____

D _____

S _____

Wednesday

G _____

L _____

A _____

D _____

S _____

Thursday

G _____

L _____

A _____

D _____

S _____

Friday

G _____

L _____

A _____

D _____

S _____

Saturday

G _____

L _____

A _____

D _____

S _____

Sunday

G _____

L _____

A _____

D _____

S _____

"Top GLADS" for this week:

G _____

L _____

A _____

D _____

S _____

Aware:

Use the space below to review your week nonjudgmentally. What did you notice in your gratitude practice? Where did you do great? Where can you improve? What were the obstacles? What were the "wins"?

Assess:

Score yourself in each area below on a 1-10 scale, with 10 being "top notch!"

Physical	Emotional	Relational	Overall
_____	_____	_____	_____

Goals or ideas for improving in any of these areas:

Affirm:

Use the space below to positively acknowledge and affirm anything about yourself or your efforts from this past week:

Week Fifty-One
Grace

When gratitude in you stays, that very gratitude flows out as grace.

--Sri Sri Ravi Shankar

I love this quote! When I first came upon it, I read it over and over again, relishing how, with just a few words, Sri Sri Ravi Shankar could capture the beauty, power, and impact of gratitude. Researcher Brené Brown describes gratitude as "an emotion that reflects our deep appreciation for what we value, what brings meaning to our lives, and what makes us feel connected to ourselves and others." You did not need this journal for you to *experience* gratitude. You have likely felt gratitude innumerable times in your life; somebody would do something for you, or you would receive a thoughtful gift, and you would feel that unique wave of gratitude, and then the emotional *state* of gratitude would pass until the next time something positive happened. By keeping this journal, you have been cultivating the *trait* of gratitude, actually *becoming* a grateful person rather than a person who, at times, feels grateful. This is what Sri Sri Ravi Shankar meant when he said, "When gratitude in you stays."

So what does it mean to have gratitude flow "out of you as grace"? It means that in being grateful, we develop the quality of being pleasing to others because our words and actions reflect the Christian theological meaning of grace--unmerited divine kindness to others. As we practice gratitude, we develop a greater sense of connectedness and empathy toward ourselves and others and the ability to act accordingly, even in the most challenging circumstances.

Several years ago, I experienced a profound betrayal by someone I loved. I was devastated to the core. I was angry and so incredibly hurt. I honestly did not know what to do. Finally, this person and I sat down to talk. My defenses were up as I tried to protect myself from further hurt. There was a long silence in our conversation, and then the part of my brain fighting for protection was overcome by the part of my brain that realized, like me, this person was also hurting. I reached over, gently placed my hand on this person, and said, "I know you must be hurting, too." This outflow of grace saved a very precious relationship. The consistent cultivation of gratitude yields the fruit of grace--and it is the sweetest fruit!

Monday

G _____

L _____

A _____

D _____

S _____

Tuesday

G _____

L _____

A _____

D _____

S _____

Wednesday

G _____

L _____

A _____

D _____

S _____

Thursday

G _____

L _____

A _____

D _____

S _____

Friday

G _____

L _____

A _____

D _____

S _____

Saturday

G _____

L _____

A _____

D _____

S _____

Week Fifty-One
GLADS

Sunday

G _____

L _____

A _____

D _____

S _____

"Top GLADS" for this week:

G _____

L _____

A _____

D _____

S _____

Aware:

Use the space below to review your week nonjudgmentally. What did you notice in your gratitude practice? Where did you do great? Where can you improve? What were the obstacles? What were the "wins"?

Assess:

Score yourself in each area below on a 1-10 scale, with 10 being "top notch!"

Physical	Emotional	Relational	Overall
_____	_____	_____	_____

Goals or ideas for improving in any of these areas:

Affirm:

Use the space below to positively acknowledge and affirm anything about yourself or your efforts from this past week:

Week Fifty-Two
Fullness of Life

Gratitude unlocks the fullness of life. It turns what we have into enough, and more. It turns denial into acceptance, chaos to order, confusion to clarity. It can turn a meal into a feast, a house into a home, a stranger into a friend.

-Melodie Beatty

In full transparency, there are times when I slip away from my gratitude journal routine, and if that slip lasts more than a few days, I notice a perceptible shift within me. I am a little less patient, and I find myself getting caught up in wanting "more"... more time, more things, more accomplishments, more of everything the way I like it. The world has a way of not wanting us to be grateful. Everywhere there are lures to entangle us into the trappings of wanting more, and once trapped, we discover "more" is never satisfied. And so, I return to my gratitude journal. I return to affirming the goodness that exists as I reflect and jot down what I am grateful for, what I learned that day, what I accomplished, what brought me delight, and how I took good care of myself. As I do this, I feel my soul being set free from the "more" trap, and once again, I can experience the fullness of life.

Congratulations! As you reach this point in your gratitude journey, I am sure you have found the magic inherent in gratitude. Through the expression of gratitude, we discover that no matter how much or how little we have, it is more than enough—it is abundant. I believe you have found that what started as an expression of gratitude turned into an attitude of gratitude, which has taken root in your soul such that you are the embodiment of gratitude. What a magnificent way to live!

Monday

G _____

L _____

A _____

D _____

S _____

Tuesday

G _____

L _____

A _____

D _____

S _____

Wednesday

G _____

L _____

A _____

D _____

S _____

Thursday

G _____

L _____

A _____

D _____

S _____

Friday

G _____

L _____

A _____

D _____

S _____

Saturday

G _____

L _____

A _____

D _____

S _____

Sunday

G _____

L _____

A _____

D _____

S _____

"Top GLADS" for this week:

G _____

L _____

A _____

D _____

S _____

Aware:

Use the space below to review your week nonjudgmentally. What did you notice in your gratitude practice? Where did you do great? Where can you improve? What were the obstacles? What were the "wins"?

Assess:

Score yourself in each area below on a 1-10 scale, with 10 being "top notch!"

Physical	Emotional	Relational	Overall
_____	_____	_____	_____

Goals or ideas for improving in any of these areas:

Affirm:

Use the space below to positively acknowledge and affirm anything about yourself or your efforts from this past week:

Made in the USA
Columbia, SC
26 March 2025

91e70abd-1ae2-411f-95bf-e644142ea6ccR01